My Grampa's Woods
the Adirondacks

Minnie and Tom Beahan
many years after Little River Christmas.

My Grampa's Woods
the Adirondacks

by
Larry Beahan

Published by Coyote Publishing of W.N.Y.
5 Darwin Drive
Snyder, NY 14226

2000

ISBN 0-9703104-0-4

The picture on the cover of this book is of Grampa and

one of his logging crews.

It hung for years in my grandparents' living room

across from a big wood stove in their house

on Beaver Street in Carthage.

Larry Beahan

Contents

viii

Acknowledgment

S everal of this book's chapters originally appeared in *ADIRONDAC,* the magazine of the Adirondack Mountain Club. Neal Burdick, editor, his staff, and former editor Barbara McMartin, have my heartfelt thanks for their encouragement of my writing.

Over the last twenty years, the following chapters appeared as articles in *ADIRONDAC*: "Barty's Girl Got the Picture," "Sons of the Despoilers Return to the Oswegatchie," "How I Almost Got Stepped on by a Bear," "Another Way into Five Ponds," "In Praise of Climbing Skins," "Easy Snowshoeing at Cranberry Lake," "Winter School Dropout," "Winter School Graduate," "Camp on the Little River," "Saint Regis Solo," "White Water Green Paddler," "Skiing the Old Kunjamuk Road," "Seymour in Winter," "Fuel Bottle Blues," and "Little River Portage."

Larry Beahan

Introduction

My Dad, Laurence Patrick Beahan, was born in a logging camp on the Little River near Aldrich, New York. My grandfather, Tom Beahan, together with his older brothers, John and Barty, jobbed a logging contract there for Peter Yousey from 1902 to 1907. Gramma, Minnie Gifford Beahan, and my great aunt, Oliva Jonas Beahan, came along to live in the log camps with them. The women cooked for thirty men while they tended and bore children.

The family never made much of this history which seemed so romantic to me after I discovered it. Dad was only three when they moved to a camp near Natural Bridge so he hardly remembered Aldrich at all. The big thing early in his life was coming to the city and making a decent living, something that was not easily done up there. Uncle Raymond and cousin Bessie were older so they were able to describe the Camp on the Little River to me, once they began to mellow and grow nostalgic.

I never knew much about our family in the Adirondacks or the Adirondacks themselves till my life was half over. When I was a kid Dad used to take us to visit Gramma and Grampa in Carthage every summer. It was just outside the Park, to the west. Their home there had the flavor of the Adirondacks. It's just that they and I did not realize it or put any value on it.

The picture of Grampa's logging crew, on the cover of this book, hung on their living room wall. Their house was decorated with deer hides and dinner-plate fungus painted with deer drinking from lakes among red-leafed alders. Grampa had double-bitted axes and two-man saws in the old barn-garage that leaned toward the outhouse out back. In the yard stood a grindstone for sharpening axes and a wooden vise bench for making axe handles. We kids climbed all over them, loving them without having a clue to their history.

Dad used to let me help split wood for Gramma's old wood stove. I carried the wood into the shed, off the kitchen, for her. I helped Grampa plant potatoes in the patch beside the house.

My city-bred mother warned me away from the neighbors who lived in a tumble-down shanty. I went anyway, which Mom found out. The old blind man telling us stories on the porch over there didn't know exactly where I was sitting and spit tobacco juice on my dainty white shirt.

I loved Gramma's homemade bread toasted over the wood fire and her doughnuts. I loved swimming in the Deer River and fishing in ponds up there. Once, we went to a real barn dance on Tug Hill where Gramma was from.

For a long time I got away from all that. Then, in the mid-1970s, when I was pushing fifty, I began to ask about our origins. It pleased me to find that our family came from such a wonderful place as the Adirondacks.

Dad had not gotten us into the Adirondack Park much, but he had taken us into other woods and wild places every chance he could. He gave us the opportunity to camp, hike, ski and canoe. When I found out about us and the Adirondacks, I turned loose on them.

The Adirondack Mountain Club made it easy to do that. It is a gang of other people who respect and enjoy the Adirondack Park and are full of ideas about ways to use it. After I started with them I began to write accounts of experiences there including trip descriptions and stories stimulated by family tales and other Adirondack lore. Many of the articles in this book were first published in the ADK magazine, *ADIRONDAC.*

I have arranged the articles, particularly the trips, into rough chronological order. They describe good times and bad ones, disappointments and successes. Some of the disasters seem funny after they have passed, others you live with and they make you tougher. Their order of presentation in this book is an attempt to imitate the roller coaster ride that I have experienced in my encounters with the Adirondacks.

I hope these writings lead you into similar paths that are as meaningful and as satisfying as these have been for me.

Grampa's Watch and Chain

My lumberjack-grampa, Tom Beahan, used to tell this story about the time he and his brother, Barty, were logging a job down in the Independence River country:

We was just a couple of young sports back then in the 1890s. We'd

been working hard and thought it was about time to go to town for a haircut and some fun come Saturday night. Well, I looked in my duffel and see I hadn't brung a tie into camp and my only dress shirt was tore down the front. Barty always was kind of a dude. Liked to dress up and impress the women folk. Always wore this porkpie hat, you know. I knew he'd have a couple of extry outfits.

There was a problem though. He wasn't likely to want me to look as good as him in front of the ladies. Well, I asked him an' like I figured, he drove a hard deal. I finally had to let him wear my gold watch and chain. I have to say that gold watch and chain used to make a pretty fine impression.

So we get into town, had about three months of our locks shorn off and got our moustaches cut down to size. We each had a steak dinner at the boarding house and a drink of whiskey over to the hotel.

Then Barty says to me, "Tom, what do you think about taking in that barn dance the barkeep mentioned?"

"That sounds like a right good idea," I told him. So we went off to the dance and we met a couple of fine young ladies and danced our fool heads off. At the break, Barty playing the gallant like he always done, bought a round of fresh cider for the four of us. The ladies seemed to appreciate the gesture very much and were thanking him, well, you might say, too effusively for my own taste. So I clear my throat real good and says to him, "Say, Barty, would you look and see what time it is by my watch and chain, you got on there?"

Well, didn't that take the wind out of his sails for a second? The gals were taking it all in too. But old Barty, he stepped right into my pitch. He took a careful look at the watch, polished it a little on his shirt and said, "Why it's just past nine-thirty— by that shirt and tie of mine you're wearing, Tommy."

Barty's Girl, Ruthie Hickock

It was a Sunday morning late in March, you could start to feel a touch of spring in the air. The boys had been chopping pretty strong since Thanksgiving and it looked like we would make expenses and then some for a change. We was feeling kind of flush so when Ray Stoddard offered to stop by camp and photograph the gang, most of us was ready to cough up the twenty five cents, specially my brother Barty.

Beahan logging crew, Grampa Tom Beahan at right in front row.
His brother, Barty, is the fourth from right in the back row.

Minnie, my wife, and Liva, my brother John's wife, were up at five a.m. frying eggs and bacon and pataters and pancakes. Generally we took it a little easier on Sunday. I was sitting on my vise bench outside the cookhouse enjoying the first glimmer of some welcome sunshine. I had been putting the final touches on an axe handle for Mike Macarthy, "Big Mike" they called him. He was the local Paul Bunyan. Always had to have an axe bigger than anyone else. Usually had a big grin on him and a wool cap he pulled down over his ears. He could go like nobody's business when he wanted to show how to fell trees.

Well there goes the bell. Clang, clang, clang. Minnie's a good sport. Guess she has to be to live up here in the woods, take care of the kids and keep us all fed. One of these days I'll get a stake together and buy her a real farm down on the Black River. She can sure raise a clatter when she is in a hurry to get her grub et hot. "Come on you men, come and get it before I feed it to the hogs, I mean to the other hogs." Clang, clang, clang she whaled the daylights out of the iron bar we use when we want the gang to move. She looked over at me, smiled, and called, "You, too, Tommy, you're s'posed to be the boss, you oughta' set an example, you don't want to keep the picture man waitin', do you?"

I got up, knocked out my pipe, and walked over to the cookhouse door. The boys were comin' out of the bunkhouse yawning, stretching, scratching, coughing, and cussing under their breath. They shuffled across the yard. There was a dusting of new snow over the hard packed dirty snow that carpeted the yard.

Inside it was warm and dark and the smell of fried bacon made your mouth water. Two kerosene lanterns lighted up the long board tables stacked with the morning eats. The kids were around the stove. Raymond, my oldest boy, was teasing the cat and chewing on a big chunk of toasted bread that his ma had dipped in hot grease for him. Geneva, our big girl, was tending to baby Laurence born here last year. She's a regular little mother and he's cuter'n a June Bug.

"Good morning Mrs. Beahan," said Bill Whalen heartily as his bulk filled the door and he nodded to Minnie, "and good morning to you, too, Mrs. Beahan," as he passed Liva. "You two are looking mighty chipper this fine morning, I trust you had a good night's rest." He had carried in a huge armload of stove wood to replenish the kitchen supply. He piled it neatly behind the stove, winked at Raymond, chucked baby Laurence under the chin and complimented Geneva on her good work. Bill was a big eater. He knew which side his bread was buttered on, particularly when it came to pleasing cooks. Minnie and Liva nodded back and laughed. Liva said, "If you're quick, there is some of last night's apple pie on the back of the stove."

He was quick, for a man of his size, quick on his feet and quicker at eating. He swallered down that half a pie in less than a minute. I knew he was worried about having to discuss the ownership of the pie with Macarthy.

Mike felt he deserved pretty good treatment since his felling record was so far ahead of the bunch.

Mike didn't miss much either. He saw the pie plate in his hand and Bill, caught in the act, made a big thing out of licking the last of the apple nectar out of it.

Mike looked sorrowfully at Aunt Liva and said, "Be they any more of that magnificent pie you served up last night Mrs. Beahan?"

"Sorry Mike," she answered "you just missed the last of it by fifteen seconds."

"Aw shucks, I had my stomach all set for another slice of it," he complained.

Then he turned to Whalen and said, "If you could cut wood like you hustle pie you'd a been a millionaire a long time ago and we wouldn't have to suffer your presence in this here camp."

In the midst of that sentence he contrived to spill a half-cup of maple syrup down the front of Bill's new wool button-up-the-front sweater.

"God damn it, mister," Bill exploded as he lunged to his feet, "I've had enough of your big mouth." And he reached, grabbing the collar of Mike's woolen shirt.

Mike was big in an angular rawboned way. Bill was big all over — big head, big chest, big legs, and big belly. The other men moved back — all but me. I was the boss and I had to keep peace. Besides they took the Lord's name in vain and they was ladies there. Now I don't cuss and I don't like much of it from my men. I picked up the oversized axe handle I'd been working and walked straight at them two boys. I guess I said, *"Cut it"* just about as hard and loud as if I'd let fly with my shotgun. They know'd I got a temper too. People say my blue eyes look kind of wild when I get mad so's they don't know what I'll do. When I was a drinking man sometimes I done it.

Them boys listened when I told them to. They set down mighty quick and et a good, quiet breakfast. I can't say I enjoyed mine that much, I felt more like a drink or thrashing one of 'em. My stomach always acts up when I get riled.

After breakfast I got up and said my piece, "Now we got us a couple of rough customers who think they can play John L. Sullivan in our fine home here. Now we can't have that, so this being Sunday and Mr. Stoddard the famous photographer coming into camp, I propose these two gorillas entertain us and settle their differences in a little tree felling contest. The loser pays for the winner's picture and gives him all his pie for the rest of this season. What do you say tough guys?"

Mike was all for it. Bill was slow to come around, he thought the stakes were a might high, but he finally did. I got little "Frenchie Joe" Moses, the boss teamster, to umpire it. He had a reputation for being square, and his skill with horses gave him standing. I marked the trees to be cut - a "V" for Mike, a long slash for Bill. Joe would keep the tally and call the time. They started cutting at 6:30 and would go until Stoddard arrived in camp or till sundown, whichever came first.

They lined up their favorite axes and started chopping, Oh! How they did make the woods ring. Sounded like a cash register to me and that done my stomach a real favor.

They were laying down a lot of good merchantable hardwood. Skidded down to the Aldrich Mill it was worth eleven dollars a thousand foot. Maybe a little competition ain't a bad thing even if I have to give up some of my pie to keep the loser happy.

In the middle of all this my bachelor brother, Barty, came into camp looking worried and wore out. He had a big, bushy mustache and black eyebrows that made him look kind'a sad all the time anyway. He'd gone out with his rifle real early hoping to get us a deer. Since it wasn't exactly the legal season for deer he used to say he was looking for sheep that had run off and turned wild. Never mind that they also turned brown and grew antlers.

"How'd it go?" I asked him.

"Good till Dick Kiley spotted me dressing out the critter."

"Hear'd he was the new game warden. Hear'd he takes the job awful serious. Do you think he knew yah?"

"Took off runnin' soon as I heard him coming up. Don't know if he got a look at me or not. Mean feller, took couple of pot shots at my backside."

How'd yah know him— other than by his temperament," I asked.

"Let him pass close by me couple times ta see who 'twas," he said.

I told Barty, "Go on, git yourself somethin' ta eat and get scarce a couple a days. If he comes looking for you I'll tell 'im you had to go to Carthage to see Doctor Lawler about them bad tonsils of yours. You really had ought to do that some time enaway."

Barty looked downcast as he asked mournfully, "Ain't we supposed to get our picture took today?"

"Yaas," I answered, "but that ain't worth trouble with the law over."

"I promised Ruthie Hickock up ta Antwerp I'd get her a picture of me in the woods and she's gonna be awful disappointed if she don't get one," Barty moaned. "I'm gonna have ta figure somethin' out."

"You be careful, Barty, we can't make expenses without the meat you been bringing in and we kind of like your company too," I told him.

He slipped off in his silent woodsman way towards the cookhouse. A few minutes later I caught a glimpse of his gray woolen shirt and porkpie hat as he headed south across the Oswegatchie toward the Beaver River and the swamp. He gave me a disillusioned wave and I waved him on.

About three p.m., Mr. Stoddard came into camp in a nice little two-horse rig. But sitting beside him was Dick Kiley, the game warden, with blood in his eye.

I greeted them both. "Good afternoon Mr. Stoddard. Good of you to come way up here to do us this service. And a good day to you too, Mr. Kiley, what brings you out this way? Come on in and set. Minnie has coffee and fresh biscuits ready."

Minnie knew Stoddard's family when she was a girl at Pinckney up on Tug Hill. She took him in tow trying to catch up on a year's worth of gossip. Kiley pulled me aside and said, "Can I have a word with you?"

I gave him a nod.

"Up to Star Lake, people been sayin' your brother Barty's bringing in fresh buck skin to sell. Any truth in that?" he asked.

I thought for a minute, lightin' my pipe. Now I don't hold with outright lying but this called for something other than the whole truth. "Barty's his own man," I said. "I know he killed his limit in season so he had some skin to sell, but here lately he's been so sick with the tonsils I don't know how he could hold a rifle to shoot a deer. We sent him off to Doctor Lawler down to Carthage. Told him not to come back till he's well."

Kiley looked skeptical, he spit brown juice and said, "Well, if you don't mind, I'll look under the bunks and check the hayloft."

"Go right on, then come in for some grub. You look like you had a hard day," said I, giving him a little bit of a needle. So we et and he snooped. After a while Frenchie Joe, our umpire, came in and announced that Big Mike was, "da weener and steel Chompion Loomborjock of da Nord Contree."

Mike and Bill shook hands and we all lined up for the picture taking. Mr. Stoddard was such an expert that he only needed the one exposure for a perfect shot. When we finally got to see ourselves in that historic photograph, I was out front with hands on hips and patched britches, Mike sat cross legged with his big axe over his lap and a manure-eating grin on his face, Bill was second from the left with his little cap on his big head and looking kind of tired. But up in the back row, fifth from the left in half profile and wearing that funny porkpie hat was old Barty. I never seen him come or go. I don't know how he got away with it, Kiley snooping around, bad tonsils and all.

That Ruthie Hickock, she must've been some gal.

Wool Mittens Can Kill You

Dad told me how in the fall of 1920 when he was 16, he and a friend, Alton Jonas, got a job in a lumber camp up on Tug Hill. That's way up north in New York State near where the Saint Lawrence River divides us off from Canada.

Dad's "Pa" was laid up so he couldn't work. Dad's older brother, Raymond, didn't make enough at the paper mill to feed the seven of them. So it was up to Dad.

Bill Sullivan, "Big Bill," they called him, was cutting his spruce and hemlock woods, one of the last stands of virgin timber on Tug Hill. Bill's daughter, Sally, was sweet on Dad and he was on her, though he told me not to mention that so Mom would hear. Sally put in a word with her old man and he agreed to try out Dad and his buddy, Alton, on the job.

Gramma packed lunches of fried egg sandwiches for the boys. They put on caps, mittens, mufflers, mackinaws and knee-high boots and took the train from Carthage twenty miles or so to Tylerville. It was an ominous, cloudy winter day, the kind of day when, what up there they call a "Black River thaw" is likely to come crashing down. Grampa had warned them again about the deep snow that blows in quick, there, off Lake Ontario. That advice got crowded in with a lot more; keep an edge on your axe, bend your saw-blade teeth just so and things like that.

They got off the train and the storm broke on them with five miles to go. They fought their way, post-holing-it through what got to be three foot of snow. Alton's heart wasn't too good, either, Dad said.

They finally made it to a farmhouse with a lighted window where a hospitable neighbor-family of Sullivan's fed them up good and gave them a place to sleep. Next morning their weight helped the farmer bust out the road with a team dragging two big iron pots. He dropped the boys off at the job.

Bill Sullivan welcomed them and took them, new axes in hand, down into the big woods where the men were working

René LaRoche and his brother, Pete, short, powerfully built men with huge black beards, were expert fellers, hungry for work. They had come all the way from across the Saint Lawrence. Using a two-man crosscut saw, the pair was dropping 400-year-old hemlocks with speed and deadly precision. They were preparing to skin off their branches with axes, do the whole job themselves, squeeze the biggest pay they could out of Sullivan.

There was not much good feeling between the Irish and the French in those woods, anyway. Sullivan had taken them on because they were good at the work and they worked cheaper than most.

Sullivan stopped at a little distance and called over the snow, "Hey René, this here two kids is Larry Beahan and Alton Jonas. I want you to keep an eye on them. Have 'em trim them hemlock logs. OK?"

"Ho kay, sure, you bet, Boss," answered René and mumbled something that Dad said sounded like "Pie cheese crust in the cellar got damp. Pa sent Godfrey to Potsdam to get a new hat and it got damp, too." Dad and his dad before him never swore. That joke I just quoted was as close to swearing as I ever heard from either one of them, outside of letting out a shrill whistle if they'd hit their thumb with a hammer or something.

Sullivan called again, "Is that OK with you *and* Pete?" stressing the "and."

"Sure ting, Boss," René shrugged his shoulders and answered.

Then he called, "Hey you kid, you, you skinny guy," motioning to Dad, "You chop dem branches," and he pointed to a downed tree.

Sullivan left them with a wave, heading, with more directions, toward a man leading a team of horses.

"And you, with that disgrace excuse moustache, you take dat one over der," he ordered.

The boys stripped off their mackinaws, climbed up onto the felled trees and, in the shivering cold, set to hacking away.

René and Pete sat down on a log and took a moment to light clay pipes and watch the fun. They mumbled and chuckled things like *sacre bleu* and *merd* to one another, elbowed and winked as they gestured at the boys.

Then Dad took a really big swing. His axe head clanged sideways. Its slick handle slipped out of his wool mittened hands and flew between the two huddled French guys. They jumped apart. René's pipe broke. The glowing ash spilt onto his patched woolen pants.

He came flying at Dad, screaming "I kill you, you son-of-a-bitch fucking Mick bastard." These were not Dad's exact words but they are my best guess of what the guy must have said.

Dad was on the log, so he had much better footing. He ran the length of the bare horizontal stem like a squirrel and launched himself off the end of it in the direction of Big Bill. René surged through the snow not far behind.

"Take her easy there, Frenchie. Take her easy. You know I don't tolerate no fightin'," said Big Bill Sullivan placing his bulk between Dad and the assassin.

Thus Dad persuaded me that chopping wood while wearing wool mittens was a bad idea. He never did convince me about swearing.

Towering white pines on the way to High Falls.

Sons of the Despoilers

In the early part of the twentieth century the Adirondacks were stripped of much of their forest cover. My grandfather, Tom Beahan, and his brothers were among those that did the job. My dad was born into it in 1904 at their lumber camp on the Little River near Aldrich, New York. They lived in a log shanty and slept in a loft. My grandmother, Minnie Beahan helped cook, when she wasn't having a baby. My grandfather specialized in sharpening and maintaining the saws and axes. The Beahans did not get rich out of it.

Dad gave me Grampa's recipe for cooking loon. "Nail the bird to a pine board, boil it, and when you can stick a fork through the board, it's done." Sports from the city used to stay with them at the camp. Grampa's system of keeping them from getting lost while hunting was to point out the big hill nearby and say, "Just keep that hill on your left shoulder till you get back to the camp."

In late September of 1983, my oldest son and I finally made it back there to the camp at Aldrich. Dad went up to look the area over with us a couple of years before that but his knees weren't good enough for this trip. On the way, Teck, as my son is known in the family, and I first visited the old deserted Maxwell farm on the edge of Carthage. It is now state land. The family spent one financially disastrous year on that place after they came out of the woods. Grampa said, "Well, at least we got a year's living out of it." We also drove by the beautiful, still relatively remote Soft Maple Reservoir where Dad worked as an assistant cook one season.

A diner proprietor on Route 3 and his wife laughed when we asked about a taxi service to get us to the far end of the trail after we parked our car. He called the garage to see if his car was ready so he could give us the lift. It wasn't, so he advised, "Go into any bar and ask for someone with a jeep." We did and it worked like a charm.

Our trip to the lumbered areas began at Wanakena where we parked our car at the head of Dead Creek Flow Trail. In the bar of Pine Cone Lodge there, the son of the new owner agreed to help. He took us in his big four-wheel-drive pickup, which he said he had been using to race on sand dunes around Las Vegas. We went back up Route 3 through Star Lake and the town of Oswegatchie, down the Coffins Mills Road through Aldrich to the big wooden gate to the Schuler Estate. His heavy-duty truck was not really necessary but was comforting on the old dirt road down to Streeter Lake. The previous day we had checked this route and there was a huge tree blocking the road. Overnight a ranger had come in and cut it out, saving us about two miles.

At nine in the morning our first day we started at the wooden gate, walked across Schuler's old potato field, and passed Streeter and Crystal Lakes, following a well-defined old road. After a bit we ran into the ranger who had cut away the blowdown for us. He was in his Jeep Cherokee coming north toward Streeter Lake. He stopped and explained he had been pulling out beaver dams to keep the road clear and he pointedly asked where we were headed. We later agreed it might have been smart to check with him in Wanakena. Still he seemed to think our plan reasonable. We told him we were heading south to find the marker placed by Verplanck Colvin in the 1880s at the southwest corner of St. Lawrence County. After that, we intended to bushwhack east along the county line till we hit Cage Lake and there pick up the trail to the High Falls of the Oswegatchie and thence up the Dead Creek Flow Trail back to Wanakena.

The ranger gave us specific directions that proved very helpful in finding the marker; he told us the Delta Club had painted the county line a few years ago. But he did not tell us the bridge over the Oswegatchie below Griffins Rapids was out.

We followed the old road south crossing Bassett Creek and passing alongside a loop of the Middle Branch of the Oswegatchie. After a bit, the trail split into three foot paths. We took the middle one as directed and then found a burned down camp with nice standing fireplace. A little further on there was an old collapsed camp to the right. The ranger said the marker was just a little way from the second camp. It took us some searching to find it. If you look for it, walk 40 paces down the path beyond the second camp. Just before the creek crosses, go directly south into the woods about 100 yards. There it is, an engraved granite marker about four feet high, standing amidst a number of good-sized trees on a forest floor covered in ferns.

At two that afternoon we started the real heart of the trip, traversing about three miles of the St. Lawrence-Herkimer County line. It had been raining lightly and the woods were soaked from heavy rains the previous day. We found yellow blazes heading east and set a compass course to help find them. The going was extremely difficult. There were frequent large trees with entangled branches blown down, there were boulders, old rotten

Larry Beahan III, "Teck," at Colvin's Great Corner.

logs, swamps, beaver dams, and most troublesome and frustrating, extremely dense growths of low young spruce completely soaked with rain. Much of the way we "breast-stroked" through this. My Insulite sleeping pad, which was rolled up on the top of my pack, was worn ragged. Finding blazes became "tougher than blazes." Teck would go out ahead and I drew a "voice azimuth" (a term we may have invented) on him to the next blaze. Many times we could not see each other twenty feet apart. By five, our rain suits were wet through and we were quite fatigued. Having traversed what we thought was about 1.5 miles of the county line and walked a total of seven miles, we made a welcome camp under several big hemlocks, got into dry clothes and slept soundly.

Larry Beahan at the gate to Schuler Tract.

Next morning, after scouting around, we found that we were at the very end of the yellow blazes and right next to a large yellow stake and several old Schuler private-property signs. We deduced that this was the southeast corner of the Schuler tract. Teck was impressed that the signs were so politely phrased, "Please respect the privacy of the owner."

By 9:15 am on our second day we had found only two yellow blazes in the easterly direction of our intended route. We decided to go ahead on our own navigation. We set a compass course based on our topographic maps and set out again with Teck ahead and me guiding him with the compass. Soon we were again quite wet and began to feel as if we were "bushwhacked" rather than doing the bush whacking. The terrain was at least as difficult as the previous day's. We began checking the course by using our altimeter and more carefully comparing the topo map contours with what features we could actually see. Things were not adding up. Then we came on a small stream, a marsh, and a hill, the particular shape of which located us a quarter mile north of where we wanted to be. We struck off south and east, hoping that we had things figured correctly, but wishing we had my grandfather watching out for us and perhaps telling us to circle a hill.

It seemed strange to be so out of touch with civilization and yet to regularly see and hear USAF "Warthog" ground support jets zooming overhead. We wondered if we were really in trouble, would they see one of our orange distress flares?

Well, the worry was for naught because at noon we started cheering as the waters of Cage Lake appeared through the brush. The shoreline and size of the lake matched our map and we knew there was a trail and a shelter at the head of the lake. It took us another hour to fight our way through blueberry bog and spruce scrub to the shelter.

It was pure delight to be on a well-marked trail again, and we started to poke fun at the tenderfeet for whom the log bridges were placed over the beaver pond just up the trail from Cage Lake. But we stopped the joking and started swearing when the logs ran out and we started wading in the sometimes-hip deep water. Beavers may be cute but they are also a pain. It was here we picked up walking staffs carved by beavers. They make keeping your balance along the top of a dam much easier. Incidentally if you try this trip give up any idea of ever having dry feet except at night in your tent.

Soon the trail improved and, about five, we reached the lean-to on the Oswegatchie above Griffins Rapids. We pitched our tent in a light rain, having wandered about six miles to cover the intended four. There were fishermen who came by canoes, set up in the lean-to. They gave us the news that the bridge was gone but they graciously offered to ferry us across in the morning. The river is 40 to 50 feet wide and flows deep, strong, and dark. We figured we could swim, making a raft for our packs by lashing together several cut logs we found at the site; but we were content to accept the assistance we were so kindly offered. We played some backgammon in the tent that night and admired the stars that became visible later.

In the morning it was clear and cool. We noted the barometer reading had changed considerably, indicating a high-pressure area had moved in and confirming the improved weather. The temperatures during the trip were in the 40s and 50s. The leaves were just starting to turn orange and red. The sunshine and open trail gave us our first chance to admire the color.

On our third day we set off before nine, waving goodbye to our fishermen friends who had, besides landing us on the other shore, already landed two brook trout. Despite the sun, a few minutes down the trail we were wet again from the dew-covered bushes. The trip to High Falls was easy and straightforward. I feel I must comment here that we were not at all bothered by bugs on this trip into an area much maligned for them.

Along the way we noted hair-filled coyote dung, mole tunnels across the trail, an abandoned logging derrick, almost-tame Downey woodpeckers, many Flicker, acres of blueberry bushes and tall stands of virgin white pine. The High Falls themselves were impressive with their jutting red rocks and rushing water all a-twinkle in bright sunlight.

We were at the falls by eleven and had hiked out along Dead Creek Flow Trail to Wanakena by 3:15 including a side trip to Januck's Landing for lunch. We went about ten miles the last day. All in all it was a delightful, challenging trip.

We learned:

—In the east, add magnetic deviation
—Bushwhacking ain't easy
—The bridge on the Oswegatchie below Griffins Rapids is out
—Beavers are pesky

REFERENCES:
Colvin, Verplanck - *Survey of the Adirondacks.*
(Verplanck Colvin's 100-year-old book on surveying the Adirondacks is excellent and entertaining preparation for this trip. He gives you minutes taken at the Council of the Colonial Government in 1771 in which Toten and Crossfield presented their petition to buy the land whose northern border was that of Herkimer County. He implies that the land was being sought to exploit the timber, not for settlement. He gives field notes from the original survey by Ebenezer Jessup in 1772 and a later survey by Mitchell for the Macombs Purchase, including names of the Mohawks along on the survey.)

Wadsworth, Bruce. — *An Adirondack Sampler II Backpacking Trips*

O'Shea, Peter V.— *Discover the Schueler Tract*, Adirondac, September 1982

Rosevear, Ruth B. — Search for the "Great Corner," Adirondac, October 1976

7.5 minute U.S. Geological Survey Maps:
        Oswegatchie
        Oswegatchie Southeast
        Five Ponds
        Newton Falls

Cranberry Lake, the Bushwhack That Wasn't

Drizzle, drizzle, drizzle! It was August. There we were, eight of us, huddled in a bandit's cave. The bandit in this case was a most persistent chipmunk who scolded us, heartlessly, insisting he deserved the place more than any of the rest of us.

The cave consisted of two large boulders securely overlapping one another in a way that provided excellent shelter. Earlier campers had set up a fireplace and the floor was covered with dry hemlock needles and twigs. It was comfortable, especially in contrast to our soggy campsite on the nearby shore of Curtis Pond.

I had just finished a good oatmeal and coffee breakfast. My thoughts wandered to the brigand's camp in the Spanish Sierra in George Bernard Shaw's play, *Don Juan in Hell*, just before it turned into hell. Presuming that the rest of the crew would share my disdain for hiking in the rain, I prepared myself like Don Juan, or the devil, for a long day of philosophical discussion in this cozy den.

But then talk made a disturbing turn to, "What'll we do today?" and pretty soon I, the nominal leader, was playing Akim Tamirof to my friend, Pauline's, Pilar in the Loyalists' cave in Ernest Hemingway's *For Whom the Bell Tolls*. She wants me and Gary Cooper to blow the bridge. No, that wasn't it, she laid out a plan for us to go on to Dog Pond in the rain, without our packs, come back here for lunch, and then hike toward the trailhead for an early exit Monday.

We had followed our original plan up to this point, when the rain encouraged a strategic revision. We had slept Friday night at the Route 3 trailhead for Brandy Brook snowmobile trail, which is two and a half miles east of Cranberry Lake. We breakfasted well at the Stone Manor in Cranberry Lake and then hiked eight miles down the Brandy Brook leg of the Dog Pond loop-trail, past Cranberry Lake and Hedgehog Pond to spend the night at Curtis Pond. That left us Sunday and Monday to complete the twenty-mile loop.

The difficulty, that made this trip interesting, was that Ranger John Kramer of Canton who had very kindly sent me maps of the loop the previous winter advised that his crew had not had time to finish the three to four

miles of trail north from Dog Pond to the Burnt Bridge Lean-to and Brandy
Brook Trail. That is what had sold the trip. We were to have a bushwhack.

Cranberry Lake

So two couples, Larry and Pauline, and Teck and Cindy, as well as
Mike and his seven-year-old son Tyler, Dan and myself conferenced. Tyler
had been a good little hiker that first day. He carried a fair portion of his
own gear part of the way but some of the way it looked like he might have
used a carry himself. Pauline and Cindy were good sports but this was their
first backpack. Dan, Mike, Teck and I were all pretty seasoned hikers. Everyone had been fired up about finding our way through that untracked
section of primeval forest but by Saturday morning the rain and eight-mile
hike had dampened our ardor as well as our socks, sleeping bags and tents.

Flexibility was the order of the day. Dan had decided to double back
the way we had come so he could go to work Monday. Some of us, myself
included, were for a leisurely day in camp, some for bulling ahead with the
original plan. Finally, Dan headed back on his own and the rest of us settled
on Pauline's compromise, a damp day trip to Dog Pond without full packs
and leaving for home a bit earlier on Monday.

So we put on ponchos, rainsuits and hats, improvised daypacks and set out in the rain. Teck pointed out the dense wet spruce scrub that lined the trail much of the way and said, "Aren't you glad we aren't going to fight that today?" I had to agree. The rain drizzled on, sometimes there was a heavier shower and we huddled for a time under a giant hemlock or white pine. There are some pretty good-sized woods in there now including beech

Larry II and Cindy from the Bandits' Cave near Curtis Pond

and maple. Some of the old dead timber had giant dinner-plate fungus grow-ing on them. Uncle Raymond used to paint them with scenes of deer. We scared up deer twice and one big bird we thought was a turkey on the way to Dog Pond.

Around the turn of the century the Indian Mountain Club had one of its lodges at Dog Pond. Fay Welch, guide, naturalist, and teacher, came to Cranberry Lake as a boy in 1903 not far away from where my Dad was born on the Little River. In Albert Fowler's collection on Cranberry Lake,

Fay described his days as a guide at Dog Pond. He recalled it as "a wilderness, an untouched and exceedingly beautiful area." Then, after the logging and the forest fires that followed, he said, "Now the primeval forest is gone from the slopes around the lake, the trout are gone from the lake, and the beauty of Curtis, Dog, Darning Needle, and the other ponds has been so marred that several generations will be needed to restore it." Well, Fay, wherever you are, a generation or so has passed and I'll have to tell you those woods are looking pretty good now. John Kramer even says fish are back in Dog Pond.

We passed south of two ponds on the way to Dog; one had an island in its middle. It wasn't labeled on our map but it did show the island that gave it that darning needle look. Just before Dog Pond we found the end of the marked trail and John Kramer's hopeful sign pointing north. Someone had hung a big old rusty two-man crosscut sawblade over the sign. Many's the time my dad and I used one of those before the noisy chainsaws came along and made "cuttin' wood" so easy, and so dangerous.

Crosscut saw blade on the trail.

We ate and rested at Dog Pond with a light rain still falling. I took a look in the direction the new trail would take toward Burnt Bridge. I suddenly realized that the clearing we were in contained the foundation of a sizable building as well as a very lush blueberry patch. Tyler and us men got excitedly involved in eating berries and sifting over the relics. There were many iron fixtures, parts of wagons and sleighs, horseshoes and the front of an iron stove. The horseshoes were immense. They must have been for Paul Bunyan-sized horses for skidding timber. The broken stove front was decorated with a deer drinking at an evergreen-lined pond.

Standing in the remains of that old camp I could imagine the comings and goings of "sports" from the city and guides showing them the way things are done in the woods and doing it all for them. I recalled that the Emporium Lumber Company moved in next. Warren Guinip was a Cranberry Lake jobber of that era. Blue Mountain Lake Museum has him on audiotape. I listened to him, hoping to hear a connection with my grandfather's logging operation. The closest thing I got was the fact that a guy named Wilcox ran the Pig's Ear, a saloon down at Chair Rock at the south end of Cranberry Lake. Someone in our family married a Wilcox somewhere along the line.

Guinip brought to life for me the sights and sounds of logging: ringing axes, falling trees, the screech of saws, powerful horses, the crude cookhouses and bunkhouses, and the sweating, swearing, singing, brawling lumberjacks.

But Pilar-Pauline, and, till then, nice quiet Cindy, were a little less interested in day dreaming in the rain. They shook me from my reverie with shouts of, "Come on you guys, get the lead out," and "Let's get out-a-here." They rounded us up and wrangled us back along the soggy trail toward Curtis Pond. Hiking without our full packs, even in the rain, that summer day was pleasant.

We picked up those packs at Dog Pond. Burdened again, we continued up the trail to campsite number ten on Cranberry Lake near Brandy Brook Flow. We had had lunch there on the way down. When we arrived back there it had stopped raining. The wind blew pleasantly. We got our tents up and dried them, as we did our things and ourselves. Then we rested alongside a big fireplace from some long gone camp and enjoyed its old view across the water with the knowledge that many had done so before.

Tyler found a toad and sat watching it as I watched them both. Finally Tyler reached down and petted the toad. The toad tolerated the attention briefly, then retreated into a hole shaded by ferns under a patch of emerald and forest-green moss on a big gray rock overlooking the pond. I might never have noticed him in his beautiful little shelter except for Tyler.

It was fun having Tyler along, not so much fun when his energy was zapped, but the rest of the time. I showed him deer track and bear scat too and how to build a wood fire. We shared a toasted bagel late at night. He made us look with new wonder at an inchworm and the iridescent lining of clamshells. He got us excited about the free blueberries lying all around. One morning, for our breakfast oatmeal, he shared out the even hundred berries he had collected the night before. They were delicious.

Sunday evening Teck and Cindy decided to hike the last four miles and get back to the rat race for an extra day's pay. At their stage of life that's important. Their move was consistent with our pattern of fitting the trip to the needs and desires of the people on it instead of making ourselves subservient to a commanding goal.

We remaining five enjoyed our campfire that night but our sleep was disturbed. Or perhaps it was our sleeping that disturbed the otters in their raucous feast smashing clams on lakeshore boulders. Pauline stayed up to enjoy the otter festivities and the howling wind.

I woke early, made a quick breakfast and packed out ahead of the others so I could spend the day at the Blue Mountain Museum. The remaining four all had come in Mike's van. They worked out a compromise program for the day: a leisurely start and another luxurious breakfast in Cranberry Lake. They remembered the huge, delicious pancakes we were served there on the way in. I had expected three, but when I saw the size of the two the proprietress brought, I was satisfied. When she brought me another without my asking I was more than satisfied, as I was with the whole trip.

How I Almost Got Stepped on by a Bear

We, six friends in '81
To Lake Colden had come.

Our start was late, 'twas getting dim,
Each took the task assigned to him.

We put up tents and gathered wood.
John took a rope, tossed high its coil.
The great black bear he sought to foil.

After we'd supped a bit
He and I looked up at it.

And where the bear bag line was set
'Twas right above my mountain tent.

He jibed at me with face alight,
"If bears come tonight,
They'll have to stand on you to get their bite."

I thought, then said with a smile,
"John, let's you and me talk a while."

Dark as it was we moved the line,
Such are friendships made with time.

And fortunate so for at one a.m.
With slash and bang a bruin came.

He brushed my tent and woke up Steve,
Gave Greg's pack a mighty heave.

Taking his booty away he dashed,
Into the lake with an awful splash.

Up on a high point he made his feast
A can of granola,
Some guy from Down East.

But that there old bear
Never mussed up my hair.

Stillwater, Another Way into Five Ponds Look Out For the Moose!

We were tired and a bit confused about our whereabouts. The sun was down. Our tent was up. We'd just finished a Mountain House chicken and pasta something-or-other. Without any prior notice there was an awesome, deep, powerful, bellowing complaint coming out of the dim woods. It put us, instantly, on red alert. The recollection tingles my spine.

"What in the hell is that?" I said.

"I don't know!" Teck responded. We froze and held our breaths.

There it was again, "ARUUUUUUGHHH," vibrating in the air and scaring the daylights out of us.

"Do you think it's a bear?" I asked in a hushed voice.

Teck gulped, "I don't think so."

After a moment I said, "Maybe it's one of Peter O'Shea's panthers."

Teck said, "I read there have been some moose around here."

"Yeah," I answered.

"One was in Watertown, last week, admiring a farmer's cow."

We quietly got up and peered through the twilight into the woods. We saw nothing and the noise stopped, for a while.

We gathered our candy wrappers, toothpaste and anything else that might be of interest to wild creatures and ran them up into the bear bag. We were glad we had taken pains to string our bear bag line, high and at a fair distance from camp. We weren't happy about going out to it, away from the clearing, but we definitely did not want to sleep next to anything good to eat.

We organized an escape plan. We kept the doors partially open at both ends of the tent. We kept our socks on and put our boots where we could find them quick, and with the laces loose. We put our cooking kettles and spoons just outside the tent so we could grab them and bang them for noise. We agreed that survivors would rendezvous at the Triangle Club shack on Grassy Lake.

We retreated to the tent and lay down to reminisce about animal encounters. Teck had seen a rattlesnake and a bear up too close at Boy Scout Camp in New Mexico. My mother got separated from us in Yosemite and she didn't think we believed her story about a bear that ran after her. I wrote a poem about one that bumped me in my tent while it made a dash through our camp on Lake Colden.

"Teck, you know all those cartoons of hunters with megaphones made out of birch bark?"

" Yeah."

"I'll bet that's what it sounds like."

"But it's not so funny now," Teck mumbled.

Whatever it was, it bellowed a few more times through the night, but didn't come visiting. We vowed to write the Department of Environmental Conservation about it when we got home.

The incident reminded me of a story of Dad's. When he was twelve, he and his best friend, Maurice McDonald, went on a camping trip. They took a couple of blankets and a sack of potatoes with them up along the Indian River somewhere near Natural Bridge. It was dark when they set up camp in the middle of a field. During the night they heard odd noises close by. When they woke there was a small herd of cows standing around them and the potatoes were all eaten up. They went home early and hungry.

The morning of October 4, 1985, Tech and I woke early and, thankfully, unmolested. We calculated that we were about twelve miles due north of the Stillwater dam, and about a half-mile from the western edge of the Five Ponds Wilderness.

Stillwater Reservoir is an impoundment of the Beaver River in the West Central Adirondacks. The tiny hamlet of Stillwater on its southern shore is impressive for its lack of development. Most of the roads around there are still dirt or gravel. We had visited there briefly two years before. My cousin, Rita, and her husband, Joe, had a home at nearby Number Four. For them, living in that peaceful and pretty place was worth the commuting to their teaching jobs in Carthage. We had dinner at Mahoney's Stillwater Inn and found the cinnamon buns exceptional.

Our intention for the current trip was to find our way from Stillwater into the Five Ponds Wilderness and out of it at Wanakena. We considered

Going through the guardhouse on Stillwater Dam.

arranging a boat ride across Stillwater Reservoir to Trout Lake, following the Red Horse trail to Clear Lake and bushwhacking from there. We decided it would be simpler to walk across the Stillwater Dam and strike north and east for the esker between Rock and Sand Lakes. Once we were on Sand Lake we could follow the marked trails of Five Ponds north to Wanakena.

I called Terry Perkins, the Stillwater ranger, and presented our plan to him. He said that our route was reasonable, with a few modifications. He agreed to meet us for a map session the evening before we were to set out. It would be bear season so I also inquired about how likely we were to be shot... He thought it would not be much of a problem but he advised "signal orange" head gear.

My wife, Lyn, came along to enjoy the scenery and ferry the car to

Wanakena for us. The three of us drove up Route 28 through Old Forge to
Eagle Bay and then west via gravel road through Big Moose to Stillwater.

We stopped at the gargantuan hardware store in Old Forge to buy our
orange hats. Don't miss the chance to visit there. It is jammed full of interesting things from snowshoes to guns, light fixtures, axes, and oilcloth,
everything you need to set up housekeeping in the woods. It is more like a
disorganized museum than a store. They even had the 7.5-minute
Oswegatchie Southeast topo map we needed. The only thing they didn't
have was a clerk. I finally followed a local customer's suggestion and left
the money on a counter.

Hurricane Gloria had come through just ahead of us. We saw several
recently repaired washouts along the way. Dan Mahoney, the innkeeper at
Stillwater, told us that night, "Two days earlier and you'd have never made
it over that old mud road. Bridges were out everywhere." His wife was
away visiting relatives and we were the only guests. He tried but he doesn't
have the hand with cinnamon buns that Mrs. Mahoney has.

That evening we kept our appointment with Terry Perkins at his house
across the parking lot from the Inn. Once we stopped trampling his front
lawn, he was cordial. We spent a good hour going over the route with our
maps spread out on his kitchen table. We used the 15-minute Number Four
and Oswegatchie Quadrangles, mainly, but the 7.5-minute Oswegatchie
Southeast showed the trickiest part of the route, in detail. Ranger Perkin's
local knowledge and exact directions, given orally, and then penciled on to
the maps, made the trip a lot easier and safer.

That night was clear and the sky full of stars. In the morning there
was a dense fog that soon started to lift and show the brilliant orange, green,
yellow, and red of an Adirondack fall. Lyn drove us to the dam at the head
of the Stillwater Reservoir. Teck and I loaded up our packs then and kissed
her good-bye. We planned to meet at Wanakena on October 6; about twenty-
five miles for us, on foot, more like ninety miles for her by car.

There were two fellows with a backhoe who were reinforcing the
dam against the next hurricane. They graciously let us walk across it and
through the usually locked guardhouse, saving us three quarters of a mile.
One of them cracked, "Anyone nuts enough to walk all the way to Wanakena
deserves a little help."

The map shows the trail crossing the river a little below the dam. Once we got to the other side there was a clearly marked sign "KEEP OFF." Crossing the grating over the spillway was impressive with deep dark water on one side, a steep drop-off on the other and a heavy charge of boiling water from Hurricane Gloria rushing under us. The fog was breaking up and the sun coming through in patches calling our attention to the amazing

Lunch at the cabin on Diana Pond.

colors of the woods in October.

As we crossed, I told Teck some of my dad's recollections of his job as assistant cook on the Soft Maple dam-building job, a little further down the Beaver River. Dad described huge pans of bacon that he had to slice up and fry every morning and all the pie they made. When he told about the story he was still disturbed about how much of the pie got thrown out.

On the other side of the dam we picked up a well-used mud road just like Terry said we would. Walking the road was easy. Off the road the ground was uneven and covered with brush. We were glad that this wasn't going to be all bushwhack.

We followed the road northeast and made a game of estimating the time of arrival at our landmarks. They were Shallow Pond, the outflow from Raven Lake, the good road over to Slim Pond, Lyon Lake, and then Diana Pond. We were surprised at how close we came at calling the times. We didn't expect our accuracy to continue beyond this easygoing section of the hike.

Diana Pond and Bear Pond are back to back across a flat ridge of rock with the overflow from one passing into the other. We had lunch on the rocks in front of a cabin on Diana, a very restful and attractive spot. Teck and I thought we might get Lyn to ski in here with us in the winter. The cabin is on public property now, but was recently purchased from private owners. It is in fair repair although the contents have been a bit ransacked by various small animals. There was a note on the table from Don and Curt saying, "We'll be back for deer season Oct. 12-20."

After Bear Pond the road dwindled down to muddy ruts, then to nothing. We found some blazes and cut brush. With those, our compass and our faith in ranger Perkins we finally picked up a more traveled road again. On it we crossed the Middle branch of the Oswegatchie five times. Most of the crossings had been washed out; a few had been replaced.

Dad had stories about those kinds of roads. In 1923 he was offered a job helping to haul four-foot pulp logs out of the woods around Lyons Falls and Port Leyden. He said, "The guy who offered the job had a Rio Speed Wagon. It was supposed to be a top-of-the-line-hauling vehicle. We took a ride up in there but he decided even it couldn't handle those sand roads, carrying a load. I had to look somewhere else for work."

Another time, Dad was working for a farmer hauling milk with a team of horses. He said, "We found a bootlegger with a big fancy car stuck in a swampy section of road. He went through there early in the morning when it was frozen. He came back with a load of whiskey, after the sun had been out awhile, and he sunk in. We got him out with the team. He was so glad; he gave the farmer a five-dollar bill. That was a lot of money then. All I got was the experience."

We followed the road northwest about two miles till we found the dug out bluff Terry told us about. There we found a road branching northward across the river. The bridge, a big iron affair, was not in place and the river was running strong and wide. We worked our way across on boulders using balancing poles. We didn't get wet but it was close.

The road thinned out again. It was more of a grass-grown path. We were looking for a lean-to on Brindle Pond. We missed it and took the cabin on Grassy Pond for it.

That cabin was well-kept. The door was unlocked so we took a look inside. It belongs to the Triangle Club, a private hunting club that owns land in the area. Terry Perkins had said he didn't think they would mind if we spent a little time on their property.

Along the way we saw deer track, and dog or coyote tracks, and droppings full of hair. There was scat full of cherries that we thought might be bear, but no confirming tracks. The sun was very low, and though we weren't sure where we were we decided to pack it in.

That is when we had our moose encounter. The following morning, Teck scouted ahead using the 7.5-minute Oswegatchie Southeast map. He identified a "Y" in the road with one branch curving east and then south. He figured that at the eastern extremity of that curve, if we headed further due east into the woods we would hit the yellow painted line marking the boundary of Five Ponds. Our old 1916 map indicated that boundary to be the famous Totten and Crossfield Line, surveyed in the seventeen hundreds.

We had used up our water making dinner and Grassy Pond hadn't looked good enough to fill up our canteens at so we set off without breakfast. The sky was overcast. The weather was not inviting.

We found the Totten and Crossfield line and followed it south. Our intention was to hit the Sand Lake out-flow and walk across the esker, (a ridge of gravel deposited by a glacier), between Rock and Sand Lake to have breakfast at the beach lean-to on Sand Lake.

We were awful glad we didn't have to carry brushes and cans of yellow paint along that line like someone did. Parts of it were steep, there was a lot of brush, there were blow-downs, and beavers had built an unmapped lake along the way. At one point we thought we were home free, then we found we were out on a small peninsula in Rock Lake rather than on the esker. We sat down for a moment. We were hungry and a bit tired. There was a light rain falling. Then we saw a beaver slap his tail and then another. Then a flight of geese took off honking in a magnificent "V". We were replenished.

The esker was not the highway we had expected. It, like most everything else, was covered with brush. There were paths on it, but they all ran crosswise from one lake to the other instead of longitudinally. From the fish scales in the droppings, we presumed the trails to have been made by raccoons. Two-thirds of the way over we found a beautiful campsite sheltered by tall, old pines, bedded with their needles and with views of both lakes from its fireplace.

In a few minutes we were at the Sand Lake lean-to where clean water was plentiful. (We filtered it anyway). We settled in there to feast on hot chocolate, oatmeal, and toasted pita bread smothered with raspberry jam.

We had found our way in. We were now on the well-marked network of trails inside the Five Ponds Wilderness Area. All we had to do was walk out. We followed the trail past Wolf Pond, between Litttle Shallow, Wash Bowl and Big Shallow and then across the Oswegatchie again to the High Falls Truck Trail.

We spent a night on a hill near to where the trail crosses the river. Between the beavers and the hurricane a lot of the trail had been flooded so we wound up with wet feet. We had looked up along the Truck Trail and saw that it was flooded, too. About midnight we woke up to a bunch of Boy Scouts coming along the Truck Trail singing and shouting. We chuckled when we heard their change of tune as they stumbled into the flood.

The only other person we met on this trip was a middle-aged woman who had come up the Oswegatchie with a bunch of kids in canoes. On a solitary walk in the woods she was enjoying a few moments of peace away from the gang.

Lyn met us at Wanakena as planned. We had our two-person kayak on the car so we took a cruise on the Little River. We had a sumptuous meal, a shower and a comfortable night at Murch's on Cranberry Lake and then headed for home.

A few weeks later we got the following in answer to our Department of Environmental Conservation query about strange noises in the night.

Dear Mr. Beahan,

Thank you for your request for information about the two moose we have collared. On the night of October 3, moose number one was heading East from Cranberry Lake after having been captured in Watertown and released at the Lake the previous day. Moose number two was in the vicinity of Constableville (Lewis County) on a farm where I observed him on October 1 and darted him on October 17.

As I have not yet had the good fortune to hear the wind blowing over a sewer pipe, or a moose calling, I can't guess whether what you heard was a moose or not. However, I do appreciate your interest and invite you to get in touch with me if you ever are fortunate enough to see a moose in New York.

Alan Hicks
Research Scientist 11
Endangered Species Unit
Department. of Environmental Conservation
Delmar, New York

Going uphill, Sherpa snowshoes are pretty useful, too.

In Praise of Climbing Skins

I said to the kid in the flannel shirt, "I'm goin' to the mountains to winter a few days. I hope to learn cold weather ways. Do you stock climbing skins in this outdoor store?"

"No we don't," he says brightly.

In a moment, I come back; "Do you know what they are?"

"Well sure," says this mountain store expert. "Aren't they the tight suits that the climbers all wear."

With that as a start, and after a very long search, I got a pair from out on the Coast. They're German-made skins and they fit my skis fine.

On this Ski Patrol outing, we were a party of four. Ahead were a dozen or more. It was dark evening as we gathered at the edge of the woods, bound for Mt. Colden. The cold was fierce. There was snow in the wind. We were there to do the mountain's bidding.

With 50-pound packs on our backs and skis on our boots, we started to climb the 1,000 feet up and five miles in.

Mike was our veteran climber. He took the lead. Then came Frank, who was new, and I was the next. On the end, tough old Bob took up sweep.

There was a new 18-inch snow, but the trail was broken, so things weren't too bad. At the start, it was flat and my skins were slow. I worked up the first sweat, called for a halt, stripped to my fishnet and Gore-Tex, and pulled down my socks. Then we were off up rise and down grade, with the trail growing steeper and darker.

Mike, with mohair strips on his skis, had no trouble staying out in front. On the flat and the descent Frank and Bob flew. But give me a rise and I could walk up their backs.

These skins were amazing. My affection for them grew. The upward incline took its toll in time, muttered curses, gasped breath, side step and herringbone. My buddies waxed and klistered, but nothing bit mountain like those skins of mine.

Seeing the plight of sturdy friends, I guiltily thought, "If these skins could breed, I'd gladly share, but in no other way would I give up my pair."

Bob and Frank switched to snowshoes but those were no match for the skins I'd attached.

We passed the tents of our friends in the fore. Finally Bob and Frank wanted no more, and pitched theirs on the side of the trail.

Breaking the way, Mike and I bore on, greenhorn and vet not entirely spent. Then Mike went to snowshoes, giving up skis, while I stuck to my skins that carried me. We fought our way upward until we'd agreed, "Enough of these tiring deeds."

We bivouacked there but before I slept, I gave them a rub, those surefooted skins my climbing steeds.

Snowshoeing It Easy at Cranberry Lake

We had planned more of an expedition, twenty miles on the Dog Pond-Burnt Bridge loop east of Cranberry Lake. But I had a sore back. Sue Kalafut had never done a winter overnight. It was January and there were only the two of us.

We thought we were going to have at least four, enough for a safe winter trip. We wound up with Sue and me. I didn't think that was enough for the Dog Pond trip. Sue wasn't convinced.

We pulled into Wanakena after dark without a definite plan. I thought I could talk her into Janack's Landing or Glasby Pond. It was cold and late so we slept in the back of the Subaru.

In the morning it was still very cold. We postponed our decision in favor of stoking up on pancakes at the Stone Manor in Cranberry Lake. The cook told us it was twenty below.

I was feeling less and less like an expedition. I said, "Sue, I think Dog Pond is a little out of our reach."

She said, "What, are you chickening out on me? I'm not coming all the way up here to spend a night at Janack's Landing."

She was reading my mind. I had to shift gears. I said, "Peavine Swamp looks kind of interesting. Kraemer recommends it."

"Peavine Swamp, Peavine Swamp, you said Dog Pond."

Well, we went back and forth. Finally she gave in.

I flipped over the map of Peavine Trail. John Kraemer had scrawled a note on its back. Sue read it with a touch of sarcasm, "This is an intermediate level ski trail. Some nice timber in the central and southern parts."

Peavine Creek passes under Route 3 at the trailhead five miles west of the Wanakena turn off. There was packed snow on the trail and about seven or eight inches of loose snow on top of that. It was getting a little warmer. We put on our snowshoes, slung on our packs and headed into the woods.

Sue was full of... well, piss and vinegar. She took off down the trail like a jackrabbit. I came along at my own pace figuring to act like a veteran Alaskan sourdough and not work up a sweat.

The trail was mostly pretty flat for three miles. After a bit Sue turned off the steam and dropped back with me. The sky was dark. Towering black-barked spruce and hemlock etched themselves against the white. It was still as a cathedral on a weekday afternoon. Sue whispered, "This must be John Kraemer's nice timber." It is virgin forest.

The trail rose a little as the creek disappeared. After the rise we dropped down and in a mile came out at a lean-to on the edge of the ice. We were on the Oswegatchie just as it enters Dead Creek Flow on its way into Cranberry Lake. I got out the map and showed Sue, "See, the Wanakena Ranger School is a half mile west and Cranberry Lake is a half mile the other way. The lake is snowmobile alley. We're safe."

"Larry, you sissy," is all she said.

We unpacked in the lean-to. The grey ice on the lake was blown bare. In the distance, under the dark sky, a snowmobile whined across it. We took an afternoon stroll to the middle of Cranberry Lake and got back hungry for dinner.

We had each planned to bring a stove. Sue tried to light hers but no luck. I couldn't light it either. "Never mind. We'll use mine," I said. "My MSR is like a Zippo. It never fails." My confidence was warranted because I had tested the stove at home before we left.

Sue Kalafut at our "platform fire" near Wanakena.

Darned if I could find it though. I forgot to pack it.

"Guess we'll have to build a wood fire," I said. Sue looked skeptical. The wood supply was pretty slim. I was lucky to find a birch stump and took some bark for starter.

I laid several of our precious sticks parallel on the snow to form a base and said off-handedly, "We'll build a platform fire."

"A platform fire! What's that?" Sue challenged. I was at a loss since I had just made up that term. "I hope you know what you're doing."

I went ahead and lit the birch bark with a Bic. I never did own a Zippo. I nurtured that fire carefully and we enjoyed our dinner by its light.

Sunday we packed out. In Wanakena we stopped at the Pine Cone for excellent charbroiled burgers and a look at their collection of baseball caps.

The Peavine Swamp Trail makes a neat little winter trip. It can be handled equally well with skis or snowshoes. And yes, the timber is "nice."

Winter outing on Mount Mouslacki the year before winter school.

Winter School Dropout

It is December 27, 1984. It is cold and overcast. There are a few inches of snow on the ground. I find myself, alone, driving west on New York Route 3 just outside the Adirondack Park. Beyond Natural Bridge a sign points the way to deserted Lewisburg. My lumberjack grampa, who logged off Cat Mountain and the banks of the Little River, is buried there. I drive in a way, following two ruts, but I turn back when I can't decide whether a road closed sign refers to my road or to a crossing trail. Everything is deserted and white.

I had eagerly signed up for the ADK winter school last fall. I carefully reviewed the equipment list. I bought food, repaired my Sherpa snowshoes, sorted through wool knickers, polypropylene underwear, pile jacket, and wool shirts, packed and repacked. My MSR stove worked like a charm. I brought along the quart and a half of fuel recommended. I ordered contour maps from the U.S. Geological Survey and marked our route and distances and the magnetic deviation on them. I switched my exercise pattern to strengthen my legs. I love camping, hiking, and being outdoors in the cold. I've been out three winter nights in each of the last four years. I have even done some instructing in winter camping.

Now why, on the first day of winter school, am I alone in the car driving over the Black River, out of Carthage, toward Deer River and Tug Hill? Why did I drop out of winter school not fifty yards out of The Garden, a parking lot, where the Johns Brook Trail starts?

I'm not sure why, but it is comforting to be where my dad brought us on summer vacations to swim in Deer River near where he was raised. Dad told me about walking home to Carthage from his grandmother's place in Pinckney with a bag of donuts for the family. He arrived home with no more than a guilty grin.

This end of Tug Hill is prettier than I recalled. Its rolling hills are cut through by the rocky Deer River Gorge. Some of the farms look halfway prosperous, but there is a house built in the bottom of a silo, a sign pointing to "Hill Billy Heaven," a grotto made of a half-buried bathtub, and at Barnes Corners Hotel the very oldest gasoline pump I've ever seen. The pump is not in service. It's all rusted. But the big white dial is clearly in evidence.

Its rickety appearance seems symbolic of my mood. I cross the upper reaches of Sandy Creek and remember that the Iroquois believe their ancestors came out of the earth here. I feel like crawling back in.

The ADK-AMC Mountaineering School has several sections. I had joined the B-group, which is held in the Adirondack High Peak region. It is divided into three levels of difficulty. Mine, B-2 was the intermediate one. We were to spend one night indoors in preparation and then five nights in tents or snow shelters along the Johns Brook Trail. Our instructions said to meet at the North Country School, a private boarding school on Route 73 between Lake Placid and Keene.

I was an early arrival. Mike, one of the co-leaders of B, greeted me warmly, showed me where to stow my gear, and suggested I try out my snowshoes and crampons to be sure the bindings fit. I did so. During the process, John, my cook-group leader arrived. He approved of the fit. He was a sturdy, bearded methodical fellow. I soon realized he was an accomplished, informed mountaineer with technical climbing experience to boot. He had taken the time to talk to me on the phone before the trip. Our group was to consist of him and me and two young women.

Soon Kathryn and Marybeth came along with huge packs and parkas. The girls seemed strong, smart, and young. Everyone seemed young except me. There I was, a fifty-four-year-old Depression baby in "Yuppie Land."

Our cooking group never really congealed. Marybeth soon talked of joining her boyfriend's group and Kathryn of tenting with a girlfriend. We had dinner together but were split up for lectures and breakfast.

INTROSPECTION

I had just come from Christmas with my family. My wife, Lyn, made dinner. Our sons were home —one with a girl, the other with his wife and our two grandchildren. Lyn's folks were there as well as mine. We had a cheerful fire, put up a tree, and the kids handed out presents. But the warm family scene was flawed. One week before, Lyn and I had escorted my eighty-year-old parents to Omaha for the funeral of my sister's oldest son. The trip stirred troublesome memories of the death of one of our own sons eight years previously. Two weeks before Christmas, a cousin who was the closest thing to a brother I ever had, had undergone a quadruple coronary by-pass. I think that feelings about these losses set me up so that I was unable to give up my facade of competence and leadership and accept the dependent role of student appropriate at winter school.

For Christmas, my eldest son gave me a framed picture he had taken of me last June when we were climbing in Colorado. There I am, in my red Patagonia raingear and Indiana Jones hat at 14,000 feet on top of LaPlatta. That sort of image has protected me against feelings of vulnerability, weakness, and need for care. This Christmas was not a good time to tamper with that image.

Backyard igloo I slept in quite comfortably.

The four in our cook group met on the afternoon of the 26th. John announced that he wanted to review our equipment, and he began with mine. Kathryn got out the winter school equipment list, and we went down it item by item. John discussed the uses and design of each item, and I learned.

A lot of my equipment was adequate. But a growing list was not. The lanyard on my ice axe was too long. My stove needed modifying to simmer effectively. My crampons required wire across the heels. Patagonia rain gear would not do for wind and must be supplemented by a Gore-Tex suit. My plan of many layers of pile, wool, and polypropylene was not enough. I must also have a parka. My prized altimeter was not admired, nor were the rubber gloves I brought along for digging snow caves. Would the individual plastic bags I packed my oatmeal in melt when I added hot water? Did I bring enough food? Why were there no pull tags on my zippers? Why did I not have a second pair of leather inner boots for my plastic mountaineering boots? One "Insolite" pad was not enough to sleep on. My fuel bottles must be wrapped in tape. My daypack was too small. My mittens needed "idiot cords," naturally. And then the girls had some more good ideas for me. I learned some things, but I was not having a good time. I was just too far down the pecking order, and like a chicken that had lost too much blood.

We were interrupted by meetings, and by lectures. It seemed we would never get through the entire equipment review. I'm not sure we ever did. My pack became a disorganized pile of junk, and I was listening to a lecture by Jim Wagner, the manager of the mountaineering store in Keene Valley. He destroyed me when he clearly demonstrated the huge difference in weight and bulk between a Polarguard sleeping bag like mine and the down type, like those of my three companions. He was informative and amusing, telling stories like the one that alleged that smaller families in goose-eating China and Russia made for smaller geese, which accounted for the twenty-five-fold inflation in the price of down in recent years. He had valiantly fought this trend but had been unable to persuade authorities in Adirondack prisons to feed inmates geese.

During one of the meetings, Mike told us he was a diabetic on insulin. He urged us to get to know our cook group members and to exchange such information so that we could care for one another. I thought to myself,

"Am I going to have to confess to these superb athletes that there is calcium in the medial meniscus of my left knee and that a narrowed disk space in my back sometimes gives me sciatic pain?"

OMENS

A few times I heard John say, "This will not be a death march." When my car wouldn't start he assured me, "You are not going to be deserted." Such negative reassurances were unsettling. I had not considered going on any "Death March" nor conceived of the possibility of being deserted, until then.

We all slept in the school gym, our group scattered. We woke at 5:30 a.m. to minus-four degrees, and then things really started to go bad.

I tried to start my car before breakfast. The new battery and extra antifreeze, which I had installed, weren't enough. Even the help of a mechanically inclined instructor with a can of ether would not make it catch; cough yes, catch no. I had breakfast with a cohesive group of muscular technical types, who in contrast to my own, fit the image of perhaps the 1980 RPI soccer team. They got along well with a minimum of words and were busy with their own plans.

After breakfast, John asked if my car had a carburetor. I thought all cars had carburetors, but he explained that some were "fuel injected," and apparently that has something to do with starting them in the cold.

B-2's leader, Tim, took me outside and attached a jumper cable. There was a flash explosion of collected gasoline and starter fluid, and with that heat my AMC Eagle turned over. That is, the engine turned over and joyously kept running. The thought struck me, "Get out of here now. Who knows what this heap will be like after five more nights of cold?" But I rejected the notion.

I needed to buy gear in Keene Valley. Tim and John debated and decided I should return to the North Country School so that our group could leave together. They decided this even though I might have saved time by stopping at the store on the way to the trailhead. And I still had packing to do. I hurried to the Mountaineer shop in Keene Valley. It was a long way there and back. I bought some useful, fancy, expensive gear, so expensive that Jim gave me a free Techna flashlight as a bonus.

When I got back Tim asked, "When will you be ready to go?" I ventured, "Twenty minutes." He frowned. I said, "Maybe fifteen."

Most everyone seemed ready to go. They were weighing packs, and I heard, "Seventy pounds, seventy-two pounds." At the last minute John asked if he could add his tent to my pack. I had, in fact, been pleased when my seven-pound EMS A-frame had been rejected, and now the prospect of adding a tent to my "humungous" pack was unappealing. We compromised on my carrying his stove. John left to go to the john without actually giving me the stove to work into my pack. Tim came by and asked, "Are you ready to go?" I tried to explain.

I had kept quiet about the fact that I had left my vapor barrier liner socks at the Mountaineer until it was clear we were all stopping there again anyway. I hurried there, hauled my boots inside, negotiated with the clerk about the vbl socks, started trimming my new, highly recommended insoles, and put on my many-layered foot gear. In the midst of this Tim called a meeting. Kathryn solicitously offered me her seat right up front. I wanted only to stay out of view and get my boots fixed.

Still, I was one of the first into my car and ready to leave the store when out came John running and banging my auto hood. "Did you leave your camera?" he called. I coolly replied, "Yes, it was part of the plan." I'm not sure he smiled. Some saints would not have.

We drove to the trailhead. I had never been there. We went up dirt roads. They got twisted, forked, grew narrower, steeper, and icier. I lost sight of the car ahead of me but made some good guesses. I neglected to get into four-wheel drive. Eventually I had to stop and back down. Everyone behind me had to do likewise. With four wheels in gear and a running start, I made it.

We dropped our packs at The Garden, returned our cars to the bottom of the hill, and piled into the back of a pickup to return to the trailhead. As fate would have it, the conversation in the truck turned to the question, "Whose car had to back down the hill?"

As we arrived again at The Garden, the rest of the crew was ready to go. I did a little work on my unwieldy pack and was asked if I was ready. I was, but I had a terrible urge to urinate. There was a sign to an outhouse at a little distance. We had just had a very thorough lecture from Ranger Pete Fish on handling human waste, so I trudged to the designated spot. On return I discovered no one was wearing snowshoes. Mine were neatly laid out ready to be put on. Theirs were all tied on their packs. I got my pack on my back. The instructors were urging us to eat. I was hungry. The only food of my own that I could get at was cellophane-wrapped caramels. The others were passing out cheese chili peppers, peanuts, and hot soup. In contrast I was discovering that you can not unwrap a caramel at that temperature. It was then that Kathryn asked if I would dig out my camera and take her picture. I declined.

We started up the trail. It was clear to John and me that my pack was unbalanced. We stopped, and he patiently rearranged the pack, which I had successfully put together a hundred times before. I stood numbly by.

Once more we started. My recently rearranged foot gear hurt. My marvelous expandable ski pole, so useful for switching from cross-country to downhill while ski touring, came apart, first one and then, ten paces later, the other. John reassembled them each time. I had used them many times before.

DECISIONS

I stopped. Running through my head were the following: the forecast for freezing rain, the dire prospect of sleeping in John's tent with my allergy to feathers and his down sleeping bag, and worse, the prospect of his having to take care of me for a week. I announced I was going home. John, Tim, and I discussed this decision and concluded that my leaving would not compromise the others, and we said goodbye. I met Mike and Tom in the parking lot, and they insisted on giving me a lift back to my car. I did not resist very long.

The movie, *Baby Blue Marine*, comes to mind. It was the story of a Marine recruit who flunked out of boot camp. He was sent home on a bus, his only clothes a powder blue suit issued to humiliate those who didn't make it. On the other hand, I think of my wife's grandfather who as a boy slipped out of Prussia with two German marks and a ham to avoid the Franco-Prussian war. He lived to be ninety-one, smoking his black cigars, and being chauffeured around by two doting daughters.

I recall the Van Hovenberg ski jumps outside Lake Placid, those amazing towers way up in the sky. People actually ski down those things and launch themselves bullet-like into the sky. Is that something like a week in winter on Marcy?

I got home. Lyn seemed glad to see me. We used the rest of the holidays to tool around some West Virginia hills and North Carolina beaches in our "fuel-injected" Corvette. It was the warmest Christmas week on record in North Carolina, a sunny seventy-six degrees one day.

Let me lick these wounds some more. I'm not done with those damn mountains yet.

Lyn and the Corvette ready to head south.

Robert Louis Stevenson in the Adirondacks

When I was a boy my father gave me a large red volume containing Robert Louis Stevenson's *Kidnapped* and *Treasure Island*. Recalling those adventures still brings me pleasure, castles in the highlands and pirate ships at sea, sword and musket fighting, and a boy my own age in the thick of it.

Today I visited a small, plain wooden house overlooking the river on the edge of the village of Saranac Lake. Robert Louis Stevenson, the inventor of those adventures, spent the winter of 1897 there, fighting an important battle of his own. He was dying of tuberculosis and had gone to be treated for it.

Dr. Edward Livingston Trudeau had established a center for a revolutionary treatment of tuberculosis at Saranac Lake, a small resort village in the Adirondack Mountains about eighty miles north of Utica. The treatment was rest, good food, and fresh, often very cold, mountain air to breathe. He personally undertook the supervision of Stevenson's treatment. He realized that this famous man would not be allowed the rest he needed if placed among his other patients at the sanitarium. Therefore he called on his friends, the Bakers.

For fifty dollars a month the Bakers turned half of their house over to Stevenson and his family. Mr. Baker was a hunting and fishing guide. Mrs. Baker was accustomed to cooking for large parties of sportsmen who camped both in and around their home. She fed the Stevensons.

We were guided through the Stevenson half of the cottage by the current lady of the Baker half. She lives there with her family and seems much taken with the lore of the place.

Stevenson was accompanied by his wife, Fannie, twenty-five years his senior, and her adult son. Fannie Stevenson was not impressed with the accommodations or with Dr. Trudeau's and Mrs. Baker's idea of good food. In a letter to a confidant she complained,

"We are high up in the Adirondack Mountains living in a guide's cottage in the most primitive fashion. The maid does the cooking (we have little beyond venison and bread to cook) and the boy comes every morning to carry water from a distant spring for drinking purposes."

In another of her framed letters on the cottage wall, Fannie complained

The Stevenson cottage at Saranac Lake.

about the bitter cold both outside and inside the Baker place. She said her husband was opposed to adding amenities like footstools to allow her to get her feet off the freezing plank floors. Stevenson relished the rough-hewn quality of what he called "Hunter's Home." They compromised by cutting up old planks to make rough-hewn footstools.

On arrival here from Europe, Stevenson weighed only a hundred and nineteen pounds. He left at a hundred and fifty-nine. Photographs show him thin and weak in appearance early on. Just before he left, he had one taken wearing a huge buffalo coat and hat, for coping with the thirty-below winters. In it he looked as much like a prime lumberjack as any wealthy, educated, upper class Scotsman lawyer-author could.

He was a heavy smoker of cigarettes. Dr. Trudeau and Mrs. Baker worked hard on him to give up this beloved habit. Trudeau knew what horrors smoking worked on the lungs. Mrs. Baker was more concerned about her furniture. Part of Stevenson's smoking ritual was to temporarily park burning cigarettes on the wooden mantel or on dressers or tables. That unfortunate trait had a wonderful outcome. The admiring visitor may now see and lay his hand on the actual burn marks Stevenson imposed on Mrs. Baker's furniture. Even Mrs. Baker may have valued those burns for she never had them painted over.

Stevenson seemed to thrive on the cold. He ice skated and walked outside all that winter. Our guide suggested that, in addition to the opportunity to exercise, being outdoors gave him a chance to smoke, undetected by his doctor or his landlady.

Perhaps he was more comfortable in the cottage than Fannie because he spent his time there bundled up in bed, resting and writing. That winter, he wrote seven essays for *Scriveners'* magazine and began the novel *The Master of Ballantrae*. For Ballantrae, he drew on his Adirondack experience, placing young Scottish brothers in the midst of the American Revolution in the company of Indians, British generals and Fort Ticonderoga.

The Stevenson Cottage Museum contains much of the furniture that the Stevensons used including a bedroom suite, a Morris reclining chair and a handsomely carved over-the-bed table of oak. My favorite piece was a high-backed desk that he brought to the mountains. I had my picture taken sitting before that desk hoping that some of his inspiration might still be lingering about for me to absorb.

Our guide was tolerant of this and seemed to desire the same sort of kinship with Stevenson. She pointed to a small often painted-over closet in the same room and said she had recently gotten around to opening it. I thought for a moment we were to hear of an apparition. She had instead found a pile of pamphlets signed by Stephenson's artist friend, a Mr. Low and dating from that era. Low painted the picture of Stevenson that peered at us from the wall opposite the desk where I sat. Just a few days ago an actor was filmed sitting before Stevenson's desk, in this little cottage, just as I did. He was playing the role of the author for a British television movie commemorating Stevenson's life and his death just one hundred years ago. The movie is titled, *The Travels of Robert Louis Stevenson.*

The cottage contains many other artifacts of Stevenson's, photos, paintings, a black thorn stick, his grandfather's bagpipes, a penny whistle prescribed by Trudeau to strengthen his lungs, a lock of his hair.

He won this battle and recovered enough of his health and wind to play the bagpipe before he left Saranac Lake. Fannie bought them a yacht and they sailed to Samoa. He lived and worked in Samoa for another seven years till his death in 1894.

"Glad did I live and gladly die and I lay me down with a will," he wrote. If he had written nothing else, that line would have been enough for me.

The desk at which Robert Louis Stevenson began
The Master of Ballantrae.

The Stevenson Cottage is located on a small private lane off Pine Street in the village of Saranac Lake in the center of the Adirondack Park. Early each September the Stevenson Society of America sponsors a scholarly lecture on the author there. Brochures and more specific directions to the cottage are available in the Town Hall at the intersection of New York State Routes 3 and 86 or from the Saranac Lake Chamber of Commerce, phone 518-891-1990.

Up at the Lake

Maggie always liked the morning. Coffee never smelled better, life was never sweeter. She had often said that to the kids and she smiled at the way they teased her about it. The old lady, if you want to call seventy old, stood straight as a lodgepole pine. She enjoyed the early morning cold, fended off by a navy turtleneck sweater and a lumberjack shirt inherited from Mike, her oldest.

With Mac finally dead, she gloated, this place is mine and I can do as
I please with it. Maggie Macdonald stretched luxuriously as she looked
over her lake from the porch of her cabin in the midst of her woods, thirty
miles from civilization and its hassles and her just buried husband, Mac
Macdonald. "No sir, it's a long time since life was this sweet," she chuckled.

By golly, look at those little whirlwinds of fog drifting along like dust
devils; you could have them tell some stories, she thought. She marveled at
the rays of sun filtering through hemlocks down at the east end of the lake;
they danced across the rippled water like tiny searchlights. The sun was
already warming the top of Cat Mountain to the west. Quartz in the rock
outcrop, where the fire tower used to stand, shimmered back. She said to
herself, "I'm going to take Danny and Jill up there for a picnic. Tough
bananas, Mac, you won't be able to tell me the grandkids are too much
trouble or it's too dangerous or whatever."

Across the lake, Joey Donaldson shivered in a damp bed of maple
leaves and earth. His thin, state-issue work shirt and dungarees were no
help against the chill air. "Criminey," he muttered, as he saw streaks of
sunlight breaking through the light fog, "Is it daytime already? Jeez, I wisht
I grabbed my jacket when I started running."

Then, with a flash of nausea, he remembered three-year-old, laughing, freckle-faced Nancy. "I never should'a left her sit on my lap," he moaned
half out loud. "Miss Carswell, the social worker lady said 'Don't never let
them sit on your lap,' but it was Nancy's idea, not mine. I got so scared
after. Now everyone's gonna be mad. Oh, God! She wouldn't stop yelling."

He pushed the image from his mind in revulsion. "I gotta' think happy
thoughts, like Miss Carswell said. Let me see now, what was the one Momma
used to tell...Oh yeah, Hansel and Gretel escaped from their wicked
stepmother's house. They went into the woods and dropped breadcrumbs
so's they could find their way out. Then they saw this gingerbread house.
Ugh, gingerbread makes me sick."

He caught the aroma of Maggie's coffee, wafting across the lake on
the gentle breeze. It only made his stomach worse. "Must be somebody
over there. I got to be careful I don't get catched. God, I'm thirsty. I'll
sneak down and get a drink out of the lake and maybe take a look." He
worked his way through scrub spruce to the marshy edge of the lake. He

moved quietly the way his Uncle Bill had shown him back on the farm before he got sent away to the State School. "Now be a good kid and do like they tell ya," Uncle Bill called to him as Miss Carswell took him away.

Maggie's steady, gnarled hand took the china cup from the green painted porch rail. Then she saw, just at the point of land that marked off the eastern bay of Lake Macdonald, a doe step out of the shadow and over the broken rock of the shore. The doe looked cautiously about, then lowered her head to drink. Maggie smiled, lifting her cup. "Happy times and liberty to you...and to me," she toasted and drained the last delicious swallow of coffee.

"Oh look," she gasped to herself, "she's got a fawn." A slim speckled fawn stepped under her mother's belly and waited patiently. "Well, if that isn't the cutest. I wonder how close I could get."

Silent and quick on her moccasined feet she moved off the porch and across the lawn to her canoe. It was a brand new solo boat. She had phoned Penn Yan the day after Mac's funeral to order it custom built. She remembered how Mac had resented her love of canoes. He'd rather cram that great behind of his into the stern of his big cruiser and stick me up in the bow where he could yell orders at me. She slipped the canoe off the grass into shallow water under cover of the big willow. She stepped in lightly and knelt to paddle a few careful strokes, then drifted along the shore, a light breeze carrying her scent away to the north.

Joey crouched at the water's edge and looked in disgust at the forest-nourished, red-brown water of Lake Macdonald. Then across the water on that point of land he saw the doe, drinking. "How can you drink this stuff, lady," he said to himself. Then he saw the delicate fawn nuzzling its mother and thought of Nancy. He stood up holding out his arms and whimpering, "I didn't mean nothin', I'm sorry, I didn't mean to kill her." Tears sparkled in his dull eyes. He jumped back as a pair of ducks rushed away from him across the water and then broke into flight.

He faded back into the brush. "Oops, didn't mean to scare you Mr. and Mrs. Ducko." Wiping his nose on his sleeve he became aware of the Macdonald place. "Pretty nice cabin over there. Must be some billionaire lives up here. Maybe that's a place I could hide." Then he paled with disappointment as he saw the blue smoke curling from the immense stone chimney and remembered the smell of coffee. "Darn-it-all, I hoped nobody'd be ta home."

Maggie noted the brace of blue-winged teal taking off from the reeds on the opposite shore. They briefly distracted the deer. That's luck, she thought as she took advantage of the birds for another stroke. The bow of her canoe created a ripple that hit the shore quickly on her side but reached out endlessly the other way across the lake. How easy this little boat works, she thought as her heart speeded with the excitement of stalking.

"Honey," she addressed the deer, ever so softly, "You got to be more careful than that. In October my Mike and Teddy are going to be looking for meat, and I'm afraid you'd taste just as pretty as you look. Look out, I could be tempted to come and get you myself."

She remembered how Mac threw a fit the time she took the 38 and went out with the boys. "Hunting is not for women," he lectured. "They don't have the instincts for it. They'll just get in the way and someone'll get hurt. I won't be responsible for it! You hear me? Now you tend to your knitting, Maggie, and if you boys take your mother out again I'll cut out your allowances, entirely."

Maggie was sitting still, gleefully holding her breath. She could have tossed a pebble alongside the doe's muzzle as she drank. She was that close before she startled them. Then the doe froze, wheeled and bounded into the brush, white tail flying high. The fawn got the idea immediately and stumbled after her.

Maggie broke into a joyous laugh that echoed off Cat Mountain and all around the lake.

Joey hadn't noticed Maggie until then, either. He froze, instinctively, as do all preyed-upon creatures. Unlike the deer, he held that position and stared, wondering at the slender, gray and crimson figure in the now surging canoe.

Maggie dug her paddle into the lake. The boat leapt forward, launched by the coiled spring of her suppressed energy. She made a short, fast tour of the east bay and then settled into a steady stroke that carried her back to the magnificent cabin that Mac had built.

About noon Joey came up the path from the lumber road that led to the back door of the Macdonald cabin. He rubbed the black stubble on his face and looked at his dirty fingernails. Gee, I'm a mess, he thought, I'd get a gazillion demerits if I came to inspection at school like this. I wouldn't mind getting in one of those nice hot showers at school right now and get all warm and soapy. He remembered the clean sheets that came every two weeks and his own cot with his footlocker with clean socks and underwear, and his baseball cards. Oh well, I guess I'll never get my stuff back. Can't never go back there, he thought.

Maggie heard shuffling footsteps in the crushed marble of the path and wondered, how could Hildy and Everett have driven up without my hearing their old clunker of a car. She had left a message with their niece asking them to run in from town with supplies and stay a day or two to help her with chores. It doesn't sound like them, she thought.

She got up from her easy chair by the great stone fireplace, stepped across the black bearskin rug with its gaping mouth and walked through the kitchen to the screened back door. Her right hand rested on the 12-gauge pump gun Mac had insisted on keeping mounted at the side of the door. I wonder if it's still loaded, she thought as she saw Joey's disheveled figure coming hesitantly toward her.

"Hello, Mam. I'm lost," he said plaintively, as he spied her arrival at the screen door, "Wo- would you help me out?"

She stood there looking him over and not speaking. That shirt looks like state-issue, she thought, remembering the prisoners she had visited at Attica when she worked with the League of Women Voters. What a lot of hogwash that was, all the prisoners really wanted was the sight and smell of women and maybe a quick feel. Well, I had about all I needed of that at Mr. G's.

Mr. G's was the roadhouse where she had last worked as an exotic dancer. That's where she met Mac. He was one of the biggest tippers, in terms of waistline and in dollars, that the girls had ever known. Everyone was real careful not to call him Big Mac, at least not to his face, she chuckled to herself. Then she thought soberly, Mac you prick, you suckered me into trading poverty and my soul to live in your own personal goddamn jail.

Now what does this sorry excuse for a fugitive think he can get out of me, she mused. She noted a kind of hulking good looks about him despite his dull eyes and filthy condition. "You're on the run, aren't you?" she said matter-of-factly but keeping the door closed.

"No...not 'xactly," he replied. "I just don' like that State School no more. Big boys pick on you. There ain' no law says you got to stay there after you're growed up," he quoted.

"Well, why don't you go home then?" she inquired.

"I was gonna'," he said putting his head down and toeing the marble chips, "but I'm goin' cross-lots an, an I got mixed up."

His nausea gone, hunger overcame embarrassment. "Haven't you got somethin' I could eat?"

She felt a sympathy creeping over her for this fellow escaped prisoner. Poor schmuck doesn't seem to be getting much out of his freedom, she thought. "OK," she said, "go around to the front porch and sit on the steps. I'll get you some beans. If my hired help come up don't tell 'em where you're from. Just say Mrs. Macdonald asked you to cut some wood."

"I'm a good wood chopper," Joey bragged eagerly as he started walking on the green lawn around to the front of the cabin. "I'll chop you a whole pile of wood. Just give me a good sharp axe," he called to her.

Maggie turned on the gas under the morning coffeepot, stuck a refrigerator dish of beans into the microwave and carved five chunks off the oversized loaf of bread she'd picked up in town. She loaded it all on a big wooden tray together with a quarter pound of butter and a can of Wagstaff plum jam and carried it out on the porch. Joey sat huddled and shivering on the bottom step. She set the tray down at the top and felt the temptation to slap her thigh and motion him to the feed the way she would a stray pooch.

At the sight of the food he broke into a grin. His eyes got as bright as they ever did and if he had a tail it would have been wagging. Maggie liked that in a man and let him stay on and on. When anyone came around she had Joey hide in the barn loft, in the woods or way back in under the house. Still, his presence could not be held secret forever. Rumors spread and they became known as the odd pair, up at the lake.

Harvey's End

Harvey let the screen door slam as he came out the back of the shanty. He finally had his place in the woods, five acres of Oswegatchie second growth east of Harrisville, and what good is it, he thought?

The day was still and bright. Not one leaf remained on the maples or the aspen. A pale unforgiving sun took none of the chill off the morning air. But Harvey caught the scent of wood smoke and a smile crossed his wrinkled face anyway. Fires he had shared at Grandma's, with the kids and with Dad, came back.

Across the yard Foxy got up stiffly. She lowered her head and slowly wagged her tail in greeting. Foxy gave up that sunny spot in the leaves only for special things these days, like old friends or the smell of fish.

In one hand Harvey carried a can of sardines, half of which had been his breakfast. The other hand held the Model 1898 Winchester passed on to him by his dad. He leaned the rifle against the big sugar maple that shaded the yard in summer. Today the old tree's limbs reached black and naked toward an empty sky.

Harvey hunched down to Foxy's level wincing as pain shot through his groin and right leg. His movements were almost as slow as hers. He held out the can, "Here girl, take a whiff of this. Bet you'd like a taste, wouldn't you? Come on over and get it, you old lazy girl you," he chuckled.

Foxy approached in her stately fashion, moving her head and rear side to side, smiling weakly with her tired body. She couldn't hear or see much anymore but she could sure smell. She took a respectful sniff of the can, licked her lips involuntarily and then nuzzled Harvey's leg.

"That's a good girl. That's my old Fox." Harvey set the can down and scratched Foxy behind the ears and stroked her red-brown fur. She luxuriated in the stroking and angled around to get him to scratch her favorite spot at the base of her spine.

"I remember fifteen years ago when you were a little fur ball I could hold in one hand," Harvey chuckled.

Matilda had gone with him to look at the litter advertised by a flower-child couple on the West Side of town. They couldn't decide between Leander and Foxy so they took them both. The skinny guy with the pony-tail had volunteered, "Their daddy was a husky and their mama was some sort of shepherd."

"Whatever they were, you come out awful pretty," Harvey whispered. Leander had a pure white coat but none of Foxy's pretty facial markings. All the same, he was a good pooch, Harvey thought. Then he addressed Foxy, "Oh, how you bossed him around at first, when you were bigger. But he outgrew you, didn't he? And wasn't he mean when he was in charge? Maybe that's why you're always a little down, like me."

Harvey felt the hurt and anger again as he recalled how Lee had died, poisoned. Someone objected to the dogs running through their yard. It had been hard to keep those two penned in a city backyard. They could dig under or climb over almost anything Harvey devised.

"Those goddamn neighbors," he thought, "I'd like to get my hands on them." His bony fingers arched toward their opposing thumbs. I would take pleasure in wringing each of their necks.

Then guilt surged over him as his mind's eye recognized the grey uniform of the State Trooper that had come to question him about slashed tires on that new Corvette. "Matilda said it was a dumb thing to do. Well, they never proved it," he thought.

"Foxy, you old witch you, you got livelier after Leander died, didn't you?" Harvey whispered. He bent right down to look her in the eye and they rubbed noses. "You know, it would have been proper for you to have mourned a little but you just cheered right up instead, didn't you?"

He pulled his head away as she tried to lick the fish on his lips. "Matilda liked you, in her own way. I guess you liked her too. She fed you every day and saved you drippings and chicken skin. I remember once though, she got jealous. She yelled right at me, 'Harvey, will you stop necking with that dog?'" and he laughed.

As Harvey tried to pick her up, Foxy let out a yelp that surprised him. "Oops, sorry girl, I know how it is with arthritis, I don't let anyone throw me around these days either."

He set her down and was silent a moment as he stared a thousand yards off toward the hills across the valley. Foxy, having been politely sociable, allowed herself to move on to the sardines. She sniffed at them, then dumped over the can with a paw and licked the fragrant oil.

Harvey took no notice. He was picturing his wife, Matilda, and talking to her in his head. One day you were alive and happy making chocolate cake for someone's birthday and then the stroke hit you. You just sat there, a dumb stranger, afterward.

They wouldn't take care of you at the hospital. Kicked you out in a week. It was hell when I had you home. Jesus, you couldn't talk, you couldn't walk, you didn't know where to shit. You couldn't do anything but chew and swallow and spit it out if you didn't like it.

The kids hated me ever since I locked you in your Ford out in front of their house. I just pinned that note on you, "Please take care of me," and I left town.

Harvey remembered his month in Las Vegas; the whiskey, the whores and the cards, the dingy, lonesome time getting there and back. You didn't last long in that nursing home they put you in. Our cash didn't last very long either.

Glancing down at the contented dog, Harvey murmured, "Well, there isn't going to be any nursing home for us, is there, Fox, huh?" Foxy looked up from her snack. "Maybe you'd like a nursing home. They stink and I know how you love stink. Remember how you used to find rotten fish on the beach and roll in it and you'd smell? Oh-oh, you smelled so bad! And your favorite sport was chasing skunks, admit it, wasn't it? But it doesn't matter, they don't have nursing homes for dogs.

"You saw what happened to Matilda, didn't you? Well, damn it, I will not go back to that surgeon and let him make me into a cripple just to hurt and vomit and sit in my own excrement a couple of more months. I'm just not putting up with this thing gnawing at my stomach and cutting off my water. I won't leave you alone Foxy, Babe." Harvey reached for the old lever action rifle. "Don't you worry girl. He pumped a cartridge into its chamber and leveling it at her trusting eye he whispered, "Sorry, girl."

Crack, the slug threw her across the yard and she lay still.

Harvey, shaking and retching, sat heavily on the ground, pumped in the next shell, placed the muzzle in his mouth and fired.

Winter School Graduate

I'm driving south on Interstate 81, just past Watertown on the way from the Adirondacks, home to Buffalo. I have hungrily gulped down a greasy Big Mac in Lake Placid and then a delicious glazed donut at Jim Scanlon's ancient bakery in Harrisville. After a week on camp food, you have an appetite for something civilized, for fat. While driving I drink from a plastic Nalgene bottle and enjoy the sweet taste of Johns Brook water. I'm not in the least put off by the black pile of forest remains in its bottom.

I feel great. I survived Winter School. I actually lived outdoors in winter in twenty degrees (or lower) weather, continuously for five nights and six days in the High Peaks wilderness of the Adirondacks.

The visual splendor of it stays in my mind and rivals the exaltation of my feeling of personal success. The forest was filled with brilliant, powdery white snow. The spruce were laden with it. The massive trunks of full-grown trees stood out starkly against it. Creeks were avenues of white with open water here and there. Their falls were covered with bridges of ice, the tumbling water heard but unseen. Distant peaks, Lower Wolf Jaw and the Gothics, were visible through the branches overhead, their summits covered with rock and ice. Icicles hanging from their cliffs were as long as the trees above were high.

Snow was in the air most of the time. Sun broke through and added its brilliance to the scene. At night I listened to wind rushing through the forest. Some nights were clear, stars decorated the black sky as the moon shone on the snow. It might almost have been day except for the silence and cold.

BEFOREHAND

Preparation for Winter School begins weeks in advance with the arrival of a packet. It contains a description of the school, pamphlets on hypothermia, giardia, etc., a list of participants, and, most important of all, an equipment list. This list is not to be looked on as a set of casual suggestions. It is to be taken literally. You are expected to bring everything on it.

I recall Tom Minchin, the co-director, doing an equipment check with a participant. Tom asked to see her first aid kit, expressed approval, then asked to see the needle in the first aid kit. When it was produced, he inspected it and commented that a bigger one would be more effective.

The packet of information is followed by telephone calls from leaders. I had calls from Joris Naiman, my four-member cook group leader, Leysa Struz, my section leader and Tom Minchin. The calls averaged forty-five minutes. They were a detailed review of equipment, physical preparation, health, and anything you wanted to know about how to survive and enjoy the experience. I thought that I got more than the usual amount of telephone attention because I had dropped out last year. But Tim Gabriel said he had four pages of notes from one call.

Looking back over my notes, I saw that the school laid emphasis on boots, sleeping bag, waterproofing, extra clothes, and adequate food. The standard boot has been the black, rubber "Korean" or "Mickey Mouse" boot. It is warm and waterproof, but it is a compromise. Moisture collects in it because there is no provision for evaporation and neither crampons nor snowshoes fit it really well. I was advised to reinforce mine with tape to protect against crampon wear and bring a rubber tire patch kit as well as many changes of socks. My own modification in the use of the "mouse boot" was to wear a thin liner sock, a vapor barrier sock, and then a heavy woolen sock. Each night I changed the liner socks for a dry pair. The damp ones dried out when I kept them under my shirt as I slept. The vapor barrier socks dried on brief exposure to the air. I used only one of my pairs of heavy socks and they never got wet at all. My feet were toasty warm the whole trip.

The school standard for sleeping bags is six inches of loft. My old bag didn't quite make that, so I bought a new Qualofil bag that was lighter, more compressible, and loftier. Down does better in all these regards, but its drawback is that in our Adirondack humidity it gets wet and when wet loses all these qualities, besides, I'm allergic to it.

You are expected to have a complete change of clothes with you in your daypack during all the hikes and activities at Winter School. This means hat, mittens, underwear, heavy shirt, and heavy pants, all in sealed plastic bags. That way, if you get wet, you can change and don't have to turn into an icicle.

Freeze-dried meals are recommended. They can be eaten from their plastic bags after simply adding hot water. Everyone is expected to bring such two-person meals for each evening meal. For breakfast we had oatmeal fortified with brown sugar and margarine. Lunch lasted from breakfast to dinner and consisted of dried fruit, candy, cookies, and nuts nibbled all day long from bags hung around our necks or carried in pockets.

My freeze-dried meals were not very appealing. I was able to force down only one serving each night, so I wound up with a considerable food surplus. I should have eaten more. I did not realize it till I was back home, but I was losing a pound a day.

When I got my pack together, it weighed seventy pounds. The school mercifully considers sixty-five pounds excessive, but with everything I needed in it, that's what it weighed. When I finally hiked in, with my share of group supplies, it came to seventy-six pounds. So a very important part of my preparation was physical, getting ready to carry that pack.

My exercise all last year was swimming. I won the one-hundred-meter backstroke for 50-55-year-old men at the Empire Games, but that isn't ideal training for lugging a seventy-six pound pack uphill on snowshoes. I switched to alternating days of hour-long workouts on a cross-country ski machine and hiking in the local high school grandstands with a seventy-pound pack.

Larry's class.

I was still about the slowest hiker on the trip and always seemed to be looking for the easiest hike. This should be viewed in context. The next to last day we were given an "easy" climb in preparation for the hike out. It consisted of a six-plus hour snowshoe hike, with a forty-pound pack, from Johns Brook Lodge to Slant Rock and back. It was a beautiful walk in the woods, but a lot more work than reading the Sunday paper.

GOING IN

The most difficult and dreaded part of the trip was the initial uphill walk with full packs from The Garden to our campsite just above Johns Brook Lodge. I was able to take it at a nice easy pace. I heated up quickly and stripped to wool knickers and polypropylene undershirt. Despite the twenty-degree temperature there was no need for hat or mittens. I nibbled and drank all the way. Joris, our cook group leader, was kind enough to say we made good time. Indeed, we arrived at our site in about the middle of our section.

Joris is a tall, muscular, heavy set, slightly reticent engineer. He has great reserves of energy and strength. He seemed willing to carry any load and always ready to lead a bushwhack up the most impassable of routes. He had an authoritative way so that when he told you to put on your parka or have a hot drink you did it, because you knew there must be a good reason.

If there was room for a difference of opinion, he would admit to it and allow you some space. We talked a lot about whether we should carry water from the brook and boil it for five minutes, as he preferred, or melt snow for water. We did it mostly his way, but to carry the debate a little further, my MSR stove theoretically will bring to a boil thirty-six quarts of water after melting it from snow. Using the one-and-a-half quarts of fuel each of us brought with us that would have been ample water, and an indulgence to my lazy dislike of hauling it.

I remember discussing with him leaving behind my Polarguard booties in order to cut down on weight. He advised bringing them to have something to wear in the tent and to get up with at night when "nature called." He said it was a pain getting into your boots at night. I said I didn't have much trouble along that line. I left the booties at the car.

The first time I had to get up at night, I had a dickens of a time getting my boots on, and I began to wish I had listened. When I finally got out of my tent and was standing in the moonlight looking down, I was relieved to

A tough spot on Yard Mountain.

see the difficulty was that I had my boots on the wrong feet.

Joris was patient with us and his competence was reassuring, but I still can't figure out why he always had snowshoes on. Some say he wore them to bed. Others speculated that he drove home to Boston in them. I could believe both.

ROUTINES

The first night we set up camp, we boiled water, ate dinner, and, exhausted, were in our sleeping bags by 6:30. My sleeping bag was warm and comfortable. I slept soundly until about 6:30 a.m.

Our daily hiking was quite tiring, so we fell into a routine of ten and a half to twelve hours of rest a night. We took our little bags of gorp to bed with us so we could nibble on through the night. I remember some of the sweetest of dreams sleeping on a pillow of cheese, dates, marzipan, and melting chocolate.

The second and third days we broke into groups to cover four areas of instruction, snowshoeing, map and compass, ice axe and crampons, and first aid and safety. All of them seemed to require a hike with a pack and often a bushwhack. That's not a complaint. Moving around in the woods was the point of it all.

The work with the ice axe, taught by Kathy Pounds and Leysa Struz, was probably the most sheer fun. They marched us up a mountain till we found a thirty-foot patch of ice covered with snow. The gang of us erstwhile adults set ourselves to sliding downhill in bunches, kicking the snow off the ice. Then we got to the serious business of throwing ourselves down the slope and twisting over on top of our ice axes to stop a slide that under other circumstances could take us over a cliff. Kathy and Leysa made it clear that people were injured using ice axes. The spike sometimes perforates an abdomen, the adz can knock out a tooth, but falling off a cliff can kill you.

The fourth and fifth days were for longer hikes. Characteristically, I opted for an "easy" one up Yard Mountain. The rest of my cook group went for the ice and rock on top of Gothics.

As it turned out, Yard was the tougher climb. The trail wasn't broken, there were places where we had to rig a rope to get over boulders and ice and then rappel down, but it was pretty. Above its rock cliffs and frozen waterfalls, the mountain was a low spruce forest all cloaked in snow and silence.

I said the trail wasn't broken. That is not entirely true for there was the track of a snowshoe rabbit in front of us all the way. The day inspired these lines:

WINTER SCHOOL — AN "EASY" HIKE

In anticipation it's clear,
Winter school instilled fear.
In execution of course,
It was considerably worse.
Our leaders were a hardy pair,
Both infinitely fair.
If you were slain,
By a seventy pound pain
They'd cut some slack
But ne'er lighten your pack.
A snowshoe rabbit led that day,
Up the most hair-raising way.
Up precipice
And ice-hung cliff.
We winter scholars fought,
Yard's summit the trophy sought.
Rewards more lasting still,
Were confidence and skill.

We had two serious incidents during the week. On the way in, the group was asked to help a young man with frozen feet. He had hiked from Adirondack Loj, over Klondike Pass, to Grace Camp, on the day before. He was traveling alone and wore Sorel boots without felt liners.

I saw him in Grace Camp. The stove was going. He was warm and fed. The toes of both his feet were tinged with black, and he was quite uncomfortable. I gave him something for pain, and Pete Fish, the ranger, had him evacuated by snowmobile. I think helicopter would have been preferable, but the visibility was too poor.

In the middle of our New Year's Eve party, someone from the other section rushed in and took Tom Minchin aside. A lithium battery had exploded in the face of one of their leaders, and he was burned. Dave Weiland, an M.D., tended to him. The burns were not serious, and the injured party hiked out with us on schedule.

Tom announced to the party what had happened. There is a temptation in such situations to hush things up. I think that, if you do, people know something bad has happened anyway but the extent of its seriousness is left to their imaginations. It is a lot less anxiety provoking to let the group have the facts, as Tom did.

SHOULD AULD ACQUAINTANCE BE FORGOT. . . .

On New Year's Eve we had another easy hike and then the party. We were psyched for the party by holiday spirit and by the fact that it was the last night of our trip.

I wondered what the party could be. It amazed me how a few simple things could be such fun. Joris wore a huge polka-dot tie. Tom brought out the only Gore-Tex noisemaker in the world. We had Fourth of July sparklers, mint tea, and hot chocolate, and Leysa supervised the making of two delicious cheesecakes.

To my surprise I found myself competing vigorously in a tribalistic rite called the Living Circle, our half of the school was bound to accomplish it better than the other half. In this weird deal you form a circle, howl at the moon, face right, crowd left shoulders together, then sit down on each other's laps without allowing the circle to collapse. We did it. Then we talked and laughed and whooped it up all night long till we were exhausted and went to bed at 8 p.m.

The next day we rose early, and our cook group was the first one out. The downhill trip with lightened packs was a snap, and our three Subarus started easily. It was a great trip.

In my view, the essence of the Winter School experience is the learning of a set of habits or rituals adapted to the circumstances of the woods in winter. Each of us has a set of rituals we follow at home. For example, I get out of bed in the morning, shower, shave, dress in a suit, have breakfast with my wife, go to the office, see patients, drive to the hospital, come home for dinner, read the paper, etc.

In winter camping, the rules have to be modified. They are simpler and more exact. You dress very warmly when idle, strip down as you become more active, stay as dry as possible, eat and drink constantly. You need a system for storing things so you know exactly where your matches are and can find them and your glasses in the pitch dark. You must know the rules for traveling together: never less than four in a group, always in visual contact of one another, always carrying emergency gear.

There is a lot more to the rituals you need for comfortable survival in the woods in winter. I'll leave some of them for you to learn when you come to Winter School.

Camp on the Little River

October 1987. How to begin this? First I must stop crying. Maybe writing will help my hurt. My dad died.

It is hard to believe that it is six weeks since Mom called and said, "Dad is real sick, come right over." I got there only in time to pronounce him dead. What an awful phrase. What an awful thing.

It was no surprise. Dad was 83. He had been real sick since spring. I kept hoping he would pull out of it. He had just about everything wrong with him that you can have. But his mind still worked. The night before he died I came over to sit with him while Mom got some rest. He was in his La-Z-Boy half-dozing. I was lying on the living room rug reading his National Geographic. He admonished me with a smile, as he had so many times before, "Get some light on the subject. Don't spoil your eyes."

I got back to my office at 8 a.m. As I went in the back door the grandfather clock chimed eight. It never chimes. We turned the chimes off because they woke us up. It was like Dad coming by to say, "So long."

Dad was born in 1904, at the Yousey camp on the Little River, just south of Star Lake and east of Aldrich. He gave me a 15-minute Oswegatchie quadrangle surveyed in 1916 that indicates the camp by name. My 7.5-minute Oswegatchie map, done in 1966, has no sign of it, except for a clearing.

From left: Laurence Patrick Beahan, cousin Leo and brother Raymond.

In 1900 his dad, Tom Beahan, along with two brothers, John and Barty, took a seven-year contract to log off land in this area owned by the Maxwells and the Youseys. Grandma and John's wife, Aunt Oliva, came along

Dad with an early power saw.

and kept house in the two log cabins, and cooked for the crew of lumberjacks.

Dad had no actual memories of the place. The family moved out of the woods and down to Carthage in 1907 when the job was done. It was a romantic period they recalled fondly so Dad knew all the stories.

Dad gave me an account of the family written by his older brother Raymond. Let me give you a bit of it:

"We children had good fun wandering the woodlands; playing around the 'bungly tree'—a huge, old curly barked birch; in the hollow, upper part of a big stump—this was our 'balloon'—we were up kind of high in it and would look down as we floated away; in summer, the children from Carthage would have plays, doing the acting on a 'stage' of old boards in the barn—Leo would sometimes be blackened with burnt cork—some would shoot off a cap pistol. We picked berries; caught trout from the dammed-up water of the creek, fishing from the corduroy road or from a raft. Sometimes Papa would carry me on his shoulders, hopping from log to log on the water. In the mornings we would often hear the men grinding their axes on the grindstone or the activity of hitching up horses."

In 1972, we made a trip to Aldrich with Dad, my wife, Lyn, and our sons, Teck, Jess and Nick. We took the Coffins Mills road out of Oswegatchie across the Little River, through the hamlet of Aldrich and camped on the road to Streeter Lake. That road is built on the bed of a lumber railroad, a spur of the Carthage and Adirondack. This was probably the railroad that brought cousins up from Carthage in the summertime.

Dad was pleased to be in the woods with the kids showing them how to build a fire, cut wood and walk silently. He certainly taught me a lot of things in and out of the woods. I wish I could have learned his friendly, open, helpful manner. I think that only comes with being raised in the country.

When Baden-Powell began the Boy Scout movement, Dad was one of his original Lone Scouts. He belonged through correspondence.

As a Committeeman, he went all through Boy Scouts with me. He took us on a lot of camping trips. I used to resent his expectation that I'd be an example. It seemed I always got assigned to do the dishes. Well, when I asked my kids to shovel the walk they always thought I was picking on them too.

On that 1972 trip, Uncle Raymond met us the second morning. He was sitting on a rock grinning, getting ready to give my dad their big handshake as they laughingly bellowed "haalloow Beahan" at each other. We walked together over to the Little River. We didn't find the camp. Maybe Raymond thought he was too old or the kids were too young to give it a hard look. Anyway we had a lot of fun tramping the woods and talking.

Teck Beahan on Cat Mountain in search of his grandfather's roots.

In 1985, my oldest son, Teck, and I put our two-man kayak into the Little River at Aldrich and paddled east in search of the camp and our roots. We went upstream over beaver dams, around bends and it was wet and cold. Again we found nothing.

We came home and talked about trying to find the place. Dad kept us fired up with his lumberjack stories. Like the time at sixteen on his first job in the woods. He wore wool mittens felling a tree and he claimed they almost killed him. The axe slipped out of his hands and whipped close by a hot-tempered French-Canuck who then tried to kill Dad.

Again I thought I might get to the camp at an Adirondack Mountain

Club Star Lake outing. I got hold of Peter O'Shea who was going to be there and was writing trail descriptions for the Aldrich and the Little River region. We planned to look for the camp by canoe. The weather turned more appropriate for skiing than canoeing and he got drafted to lead a hike up Cat Mountain. I went along with him. I have a contract my grandfather signed to log off the north side of that mountain. Nature seems to have repaired the damage pretty well.

In early fall of 1987 Teck and I and a group of friends made another trip to Five Ponds. The trees were in magnificent color. The sun shined on us and we spent two nights at incomparable Glasby pond in the shadow of Cat Mountain. I was unable to persuade the group to stretch one of our side hikes down to Big Deer Pond. It was the home of the guide, Philo Scott, whom Irving Bachelor made immortal in his novel, *Emperor of the Woods*. Dad read it a long time ago and handed it on to me along with the original version of *Hopalong Cassidy*.

This trip Bernie Suskavitch, the ranger at Wanakena, told us of a new ski trail out of the backside of Star Lake that could get us near the camp. We were short of time so we weren't able to try it.

A few days later Peter Gillespie, who had been on the Glasby Pond trip, showed me an old map that had a trail crossing the river just at the Yousey camp, Raymond's corduroy road. If we could find remnants of the road and follow it to the river, we would have the camp pinpointed.

With this new information we were eager to continue the search. It seemed a fitting quest to honor my dad.

The next weekend Lyn, Teck, my mother and I drove to Cranberry Lake and took a room at the Inn. The weather was overcast and many trees were barren, there was a little somber yellow and brown, no flaming red. The life was gone out of the woods, as if to symbolize Dad's passing.

We woke in the morning to an inch and a half of snow. Snow clung to each tree limb and remaining leaf. The woods were reborn in another spectacular mood.

Teck and I suited up with Gore-Tex. I wore polypropylene under it. He wore cotton and too much else. Teck wound up soaked with sweat, but learned a good lesson.

We picked up that ski trail. It led us over the Andrew Schuler Bridge to the south side of the Little River. We followed a trail west and then struck north through the bush toward the clearing on our map where the camp had been. We crossed a ridge and found ourselves on a side hill along the river. We dropped down to the river twice. The second time we were there.

It was Teck's good eye that interpreted the topo map and found the way. It was also he that spotted the little creek that Raymond called "Beahan Creek" and the big iron sleigh runner buried under a tree. I found the whiskey bottle Grampa might have hidden after Gramma put him on the wagon. It was behind a big square clearing that must have been the barn.

Raymond said there was also a root house, a sleeping camp for the men and two cabins for the families. We found rocks, laid out square, probably foundations. Snow obscured things but we were exceedingly pleased to have found the place.

In my mind's eye I could see the camp alive. Log cabins, smoke coming out the chimneys, children playing in the yard, Grampa sharpening a saw. Gramma hanging up wash, the ring of axes and smell of pine and kerosene in the air. "By gol," as they would say, I wish we could all be there together. Wouldn't that be some kind of heaven?

Four generations of Larry Beahans, 1980

Taste of Death

Fiction based on the death of one of my three sons.

Everett Burke was a wild old hell-raising buddy of mine from The Mountaineers. He was dean of our rock climbers' contingent. Totally bald since a kid, he had taken a lot of razzing. He liked to say he gave up wearing a beard because people complained he looked like he had his head on upside down.

You knew as soon as you talked to him, that this was not a guy whose bluff you'd want to call. He'd try anything.

We both belonged to The Mountaineers a good long time. We had some excellent trips together. I stayed away from his more vertical ones. I never could see much fun in betting your life on whether or not you could chin yourself on a 1,500-foot rock ledge.

He was a hero to our younger members. At fifty-three he could still lead them up rock faces that made me nervous to photograph. He could also, he thought, drink anyone, anyone at all, under the table.

It was Everett's idea that we replace the old lean-to up in White Pass.

At the executive committee meeting of The Mountaineers, the club treasurer threatened to put the kibosh on the plan. He said, "Sorry guys, the State Forest Service wants a thousand bucks up front to pay for materials and we are tapped out."

My mind drifted, then lurched to a halt on an awful memory. February, fourteen years ago. The phone rang at 2:30 a.m. It was a sheriff's deputy calling from Denver. He was in a hospital emergency room. "They were camped up by the river. It was real cold. The wind was blowin' something fierce too, you know. We had a lot of snow here lately and, well, I guess—."

It took three minutes, that felt like three days, for him to get it out— that the boy, that our boy, that Zack was dead.

Mary and I sat on the floor, held each other and rocked and cried. His brothers Tom and Matt stood by in pajamas not believing, trying to understand and crying too.

After the ordeal of getting him home, the wake and then the funeral we were stunned and apathetic. We talked of some sort of outdoor memorial for Zack, but went nowhere with it.

I hired a private investigator in Denver to go over the facts. I thought of revenge. Maybe I should sue the school. I felt like taking a crowbar out there and breaking legs. How could they let him die? But the feelings sank with me into a dead pool of malaise and distraction.

Mary got sick. She blamed me. I blamed her. We each silently blamed ourselves. She talked to a divorce lawyer, a former friend of mine. I started playing the horses and losing.

Then gradually our world righted itself in a gray empty way. Mary could smile occasionally and we enjoyed some things together — movies, the colors of autumn.

"Congenial" fireplace gone cold and lonely. The place where the boy died way out west.

Zack loved wild country. He was kind of wild too. Maybe a little like Everett, but without Everett's dumb luck.

Zack was skinnier and shorter than his two brothers. I remember how frail he felt when I picked him up for a hug at five or six. He made up for his size with buzzsaw intensity and daring.

As a tiny kid, he'd astonish a pool full of people and us by jumping from the highest diving platform. As he grew, he kept us proud but worried with his all-weather, no-hands style of skiing, climbing, and living.

I wondered what made him act so fearlessly. I wondered, what could

I have done to let him know that he didn't have to try that hard.

Mary said, "He just wanted to keep up with you and his brothers."

Was he afraid of competing with us? The three boys and I did all kinds of stuff, in boats, on skis, underwater, wrestling, running, playing chess and cards. I thought we were having fun.

I didn't like losing ground against them. As they ripened, I could feel my own body start to rot.

"Well, we don't have to worry about him anymore," Mary would sigh.

Zack's Place, I thought, a lean-to in a mountain pass, that would be the way to remember him. Maybe his spirit would spend some of his time, some of his eternity there.

I said to Mary, "A thousand dollars for a hand-built cedar lean-to is a real bargain. Zack would love the price."

"He was careful with a dollar. I guess he learned something from me," Mary answered.

The club was pleased with our offer to finance the lean-to as a memorial for Zack. "Gees, I never knew no philanthropist before," cracked Everett in his

A fire of rotten lean-to logs in an ice-covered forest.

best mountain speak. "Thank you Mister Rocky feller— but you still gotta' bring your sledge."

That December weekend was wet and cold. It's good for us that it rained slush all week, I thought, it'll be safe for the fire. It seems fitting that the trip will be hard.

The trees glittered in their ice sheaths. There was an inch of crust on the snow. The frozen rain raised hell on the highway. Cars skidded all over. I counted three tractor-trailers off the road. One double header on its back in the median looked like a twisted frozen lizard, its wheels clawing the air.

What a fire we had with the logs of the old lean-to. Flames must have been twenty, thirty feet high. So hot after awhile you couldn't get near it to put more on. What a job digging the lean-to out from under eight foot of snow and frozen slush. Swinging mattocks and sledge hammers all day, like they used to say in the woods, "We earned our beans."

That poor furry little brown mouse. After the chainsaw ripped through his nest, he ran to the end of the last rafter and huddled there, terrified, suspended in mid-air. We all froze a moment too, until a ranger scooped him off to safety in the woods.

Why couldn't I have been there to save Zack? "Just a skinny nervous kid, he didn't know what he did." That stupid abortion of a rhyme kept going through my head. Was he lonesome or was he just showing off? How could my kid be so stupid? God damn, whose fault was it?

We spent two cold nights camped out in snow in the parking lot at the foot of White Pass. It must have got down to ten below during the night. It warmed up some during the day, especially when we were hauling out the old asphalt shingles.

That night some of the guys felt they worked hard enough that they deserved a few drinks. They went into town and got blasted. No one got hurt, thank God.

In June we built the new lean-to. The rangers prefabricated the whole thing out back of their headquarters and then took it apart like a Lincoln Log set. A helicopter dropped the pieces up in the pass for us to put back together.

The same bunch of hard workers that were there in the winter came with us again. A few of them were just kids. They hoisted logs, pounded spikes and laid shingles so that it was livable and beautiful before dark. What a pleasure to watch the place blossom out of our sweat.

In the late afternoon someone broke out the beer. There was a happy water fight down in the creek. They had lots of fun shouting and laughing

Spring, building a new lean-to.

and drinking. A guy got hit in the head with a rock. He thought it was a big joke except for his bloody shirt.

About 8:30 we declared the work on the lean-to done. We packed up our tools and started dinner.

Oh-ho-ho, what is this? Old Everett Burke, stalwart worker and backbone of the project, had quit early, hiked all the way to town for four pizzas and another case of beer and carried them back to us. He was greeted with unceremonious joy.

I had misgivings about more beer coming into camp, but I couldn't refuse one can with a slice of Everett's hard-won pizza.

I gave him a couple of congratulatory back slaps, but my heart wasn't in it.

In a while we went down to the old fire site and, this time, lit just a little one. The State Forest Commissioner got upset about air pollution after our last glorious blaze.

The rangers had all packed out to their wives and homes long before the fire crackled and the booze began to flow.

What do you know but someone finds three quarts of Jack Daniels in his pack and someone else a fifth of schnapps? As they got drunker and drunker I listened to some more or less coherent stories about turkey hunting and then some incomprehensible ones about I don't know what.

Everett stumbled up to me deep in his cups. "Hank, I want— tell you, I want tooo tell you —You know what I mean— hee, hee. Hank, he mus'a been a goo- kid. You know ho, ho I got to go over here and tell them someth —scuse me please, I got to pee first."

I wanted to talk to my drunken buddy, but I couldn't make myself do it. The poor dumb bastard's brain's not here anyway, I thought.

I went up to the lean-to and slept on the fresh pine boards of its floor. The rest of them went on drinking. They drank as competitively as they played their mountain games.

Everett walked out in the dark "drunk as a skunk." The rest fell asleep where they lay or woke the sleeping as they banged about looking for gear.

Maybe I'm damned for it but I prayed. I asked God to let us find Everett, on our way out in the morning, face down, drowned in trail mud and vomit.

Everett was a hero to these kids. He made me want to puke — or crack skulls. He had a chance there to teach a real lesson, but instead he stumbled out alive.

The whole time a guilty memory hung over me. I used to brag about drinking. Like the night in law school at a pre-dance cocktail party, I drank twenty-three daiquiris, because our rival fraternity was paying. Our plan was to drink them into bankruptcy. That used to seem pretty funny. God, I hope the kids never heard me tell it.

A week after we built the lean-to I was back again in White Pass, this time, alone. Shreds of bark still clung to its brown logs not yet weathered gray. A blue-veined, spotted, old hand, I could not believe was mine, wiped away tears. All I could think to do was curse.

Croaking up out of my sour stomach came:

"TAKE A DRINK HERE AND TASTE DEATH IN EVERY DRINK YOU TAKE AFTERWARD.

THE DEVIL AND I'LL SEE TO IT. AND BE DAMMED TO YA ."

It didn't thunder across the valley or echo off the cliffs the way I wanted it to. But it did something for the rage in my gut.

I looked around the white birch forest with its bright trees hung in shrouds of their own bark. Their whiteness seemed unreal. I was scared for a moment. Till I thought, why should I be afraid?

Let them fear me now. I'm done with life. I'll be the specter.

Who believes in curses anyway? I thought, but what if curses work? Some nasty part of me was amused. I laughed out-loud and cried as I swore, "GOD DAMN YOU ALL."

"You're off your rocker," I mumbled to myself. I tried physically to throw off the weird mood. The hard shake of my head and shoulders hurt my joints.

Come on, let's get down to business, I thought. Where'd I put that thing? I searched my pockets and found the old ski pass, Zack's image preserved forever in plastic. I buried it beside a boulder a few yards away.

The lean-to stood in its white forest, above a stream paved in mossy gray rock and lined with green. I cleared my throat and said softly " Well Zack, did you ever see a place so pretty? We'll be coming up to visit."

The grim vision of Zack dying far from home in a grove of giant pines stays with me too. There he is with a group of buddies around a congenial fire. Laughing, as he chugalugs a full quart of whiskey a few seconds faster than his friend who miraculously did not die.

Five thousand people, most of them young, died again that year, as they do every year, like Zack, of acute, uncomplicated alcohol poisoning. God damn the waste!

Jack Armstrong's Kid

My dad is Jack Armstrong. They used to call him, "The All American Boy." That's what he wanted me to be, too. I'm sorry. I couldn't do it his way. "I had to be me." Me and Sinatra, we had to be us. That's the reason I moved out of state. Sure Dad and I miss each other. Once in a while we connect. But it's not easy. Like...

AT HOME

The old man gives me a call, "How about a ninety-mile canoe marathon?" he says. Ninety miles? In three days? I've never even heard of such a thing. What's he up to here? Is he trying to be buddies again or is he still trying to prove he's twice the man I am? OK, I'm game. I can take it if you can, old man.

IN THE CAR

Wouldn't you know it. I'm halfway there and the front end goes on my old Honda. Dad warned me about the tires. He'll think I did this on purpose. There he'll be with all his friends and his expensive new racing canoe. They'll be all ready to start this big race and I've got to call him and tell him, "Sorry Pop, some other time. OK?"

He's probably been out paddling every day all summer to get in shape. He's gotta prove he's such a specimen.

He'd strangle me if I was within reach. No, he wouldn't. He'd put a guilt trip on me that would keep me in bed for a week.

AT A GARAGE

"Hello, hello, operator, are you there? Well, yes, it is a kind of an emergency. I'm calling from a public phone... That's why I dialed 911...Yes, yes, OK. My name is Mike Armstrong...Yes, my address is...what do you need all this stuff for? I just want an operator to help make a collect call...Yes, I have a charge card...I can't remember the PIN number...Well pardon me...I didn't know that. She hung up. Ah, heck with it. I'll call from home."

Joe, this garage guy in this little jerkwater town I'm calling from, says the tires will get me home, but get new tie rods as soon as possible. It's a good thing that he had trouble with the phone, too. He couldn't get through to MasterCard. I think I'm over the limit.

BACK HOME ON THE PHONE

"Hi, Dad? Yeah, it's me, Mike....Why, I'm home. Look Dad, I was halfway there and the car broke down."

He's taking it hard but trying not to show it. He wants to know why I didn't call earlier. He says I should know I can call collect anytime. That's why he put me on the Universal AT&T MasterCard.

"There's no way I can make the race now, Dad. Why don't you come up for the weekend and we'll just lay around and relax. You can play with the dog. We'll go for a swim. Maybe we could practice a little with your new boat in Lake Kochogee."

I'm doing everything I can to assuage him but he stays just kind of glum. "OK, so you'll think about it and let us know? OK, bye." He hung up kind of abruptly there.

I'm reading the Sunday funnies. Up the driveway comes my dad, Jack Armstrong. He's got his big new Chrysler Sport Van with this radical-looking racing canoe lashed on top. "Hi, Dad. We weren't expecting you. Say, that's some boat you got there."

"Hi, Mike, good to see you," he says climbing down from the van. We shake hands in the big way they always do in his family, the Armstrongs. My brothers and I could never get the handshake to work quite the way he and his brothers did it. We did a good spoof on it though.

He tells me he paddled the first day of the race by himself but with that big tandem boat he couldn't keep up. I suppose I'm supposed to feel sorry for him.

He hung around the race a little, he says, then he decided to take me up on the "invite." Never mind that Tish and I had made plans for dinner out and a movie.

So he takes us out to this fancy place and insists on paying the bill. He won't stay overnight in our house. He says the dog dander bothers his asthma. He wants to go on a hike tomorrow. I had arranged the day off for the race so I guess there's no way out of it.

TRAIL HEAD

Here we are at the trailhead to Nye Mountain. Would you believe it? Dad belongs to a club that actually owns the trailhead.

Nye is one of forty-six mountains in New York State over 4,000 feet. Dad wants to climb all of them so he can be in another club, the Forty-sixers. They keep registers on the tops of the mountains. You have to sign in to prove you were there. Now isn't that a dumb idea?

Well, I've got him this time. I've been hiking and climbing hills with Clara, that's my pooch, all the time he's been sitting in that canoe paddling. We'll see who's twice the man at this.

People say Dad and I look a lot alike. Today we don't. I'm stripped down to Rebocks, T-shirt, and hiking shorts, for speed. I've got a canteen and lunch in a fanny pack. He's dressed for the Arctic and loaded for bear. Long woolen pants, hiking boots, gaiters, broad brimmed hat and woolen shirt. He's got a backpack full of rain gear, bivey sack, water filter, two days rations and who knows all what else.

"Where you goin', Dad, Everest or McKinley?"

"Where you headed, kid, Waikiki?"

Clara's running all over, sniffing this way and that. Then she comes back to us wagging her tail, looking eager. She's ready.

"You got a leash for the dog?" Dad asks.

"She's OK on the trail. She never bothers anyone."

"We're starting out on my club's property. The club has a rule. All pets must be on a leash. I'm a club Governor and if Clara gets caught off leash it's going to be very embarrassing."

So, I appease him. He gives me a piece of line out of his pack and I tie poor Clara on to one end of it. She doesn't like it, but she likes standing still even less. She jumps up and down, strains at the leash and barks the command at us, "C'mon, you guys, hit the trail. I smell all kinds of interesting stuff. C'mon, hurry up."

ON THE TRAIL

I notice Dad's got this big guidebook. "Dad, what's that for? Aren't the map and all these trail signs good enough? And what in the world do you need those gaiters for?"

"They keep my pants clean and keep the bugs out."

"You're going to be too hot in five minutes. There aren't any bugs the end of August. Why can't you send the pants to the cleaners?"

"Maybe you're right about the book," he says. "I'll hide it somewhere along here. We can pick it up on the way out." He was coming my way a little for a change. I didn't bug him any more about the gaiters, though they were a little embarrassing.

GOING UPHILL

He's navigating back there with his map and compass. Clara and I are just moving out along the trail. We stop every few minutes to let him catch up. He's sweating and getting his wind up on the steep parts. What's this, he's sitting down on a rock, pushing down those gaiters and rolling up his pants?

"Getting kind of warm," he says, with a smile.

I could play it cool here but I don't want to. "I told you so, I told you those gaiters were too much."

"Yeah, but I can pull them up and roll my pants down again as soon as it gets cold," he says not giving an inch.

OK, mister smart guy, let's see what kind of shape you're in then, I say to myself and take off up the trail.

IN THE BUSH

Now we are at the trail-less final section of Nye Mountain. I better let him catch up.

He's got that map out again. "Now the way it looks to me, we are at this shoulder right here. The guidebook said there were several false herd paths through this scrub. They say to take the one at the south end of the swamp on this shoulder. It heads up at 320 degrees."

"If you say so, Dad, but it looks to me that if we just went straight up we'd get there."

I got to admit this brush is tough and there are all kinds of blown down trees. Walking up this mountain is getting more and more complicated.

It's almost three o'clock. We've been walking since ten. I'm getting a little tired and I just got stuck in the eye with a stick. Dad got the remnants out for me by flipping my eyelid and dabbing with a bandanna. He got stung by a bee. I found some jewelweed to put on it for him.

"Where do you think the top of this mountain is, Pop?"

"Damned if I know. None of these paths seem to go anywhere but around in circles. This map is no help at all up here."

Clara perks her ears up and looks ahead. "She hears something," Dad says.

I hear it, too. "Someone's coming down," I say.

"Yeah, sounds like they're laughing."

Here they come: three young ladies and a dog. Clara and their dog immediately sniff each other over and start playing games. I'm out ahead of Dad so I'm next to meet them.

"Hi, did you get to the top?" I ask.

Dad hurries up with his big friendly non-family smile. "Nice to see you girls. Beautiful day for hiking isn't it. Did you come in at our club's trail head?"

The tall blonde, with the bandanna sweatband takes a second and decides to answer me instead of Dad. The three of them are feeling good. "Yeah, we found it, finally," she laughs.

"This is our third trip and we finally found the damn Forty-sixer canister," chimes in the slender short girl in the red plaid shirt.

"So, we're all signed in," the plump one shouts and laughs. They are kind of hyper, wound up about getting to the top, I guess.

"Ye-ah-hoo," the little one whoops. She comes running at me yelling, "We swore we were gonna' kiss the first good looking guy we found coming down, no matter what he said." She brushes by the blonde. "You're it," she yells. She plants a big wet kiss on me and then they pass me on one to the other.

I kind of like this.

The girls keep right on going, laughing down the hill.

Dad doesn't get a tumble. "You ain't got sex appeal, Pop."

"Apparently not," he sighs.

"Hey girls, help us out," Dad calls. "Which way is the top?"

"Find it yourself. We're not telling," they laugh back.

"I've about had it," he says

The poor old bastard looks broken. I notice that the stubble of his beard is mostly gray. The lines in his face are getting deeper. I feel bad about the canoe race and now it looks as if he isn't even going to get to the top of Nye Mountain.

"Naw, come on Dad, it's got to be around here somewhere. Let's find it." I give him one of my chocolate bars. We drink up the last of his water. We take one more squint at the map. Then we start busting into the spruce brush in the direction from which those vengeful Sabine women had come.

Clara is out in front but now she is purposeful. I want to go one way; she wants to go another. She insists.

"Do you think she's following their scent?" asks Dad.

"I don't know. Maybe. She's always chasing stuff but I didn't think she had any bloodhound in her," I say.

AT THE TOP

Half an hour later here we are sitting in the middle of a jungle on top of Nye Mountain. There is absolutely no view but there is a Forty-sixer canister.

Clara is lying flat out with most of her tongue exposed for extra cooling. Dad has the sign-in book in his hand and is reading. I'm putting some moleskin from Dad's first aid kit over a blister on my heel.

"Meagan, Flora and Tootles, here's where they signed in," he crows. "Here they are, all three of your girlfriends. Do you want their addresses? Here, I'll copy them down for you. Wait till I tell Tish."

"You ain't tellin' nothin', old man. You're just mad that none of them were senior citizens. You tell anyone and I won't loan you my dog to get up any more of these mountains. Then you'll never get into that Forty-sixer thing."

We laugh and shake hands. We'll probably do this again.

Winter Leadership School in the Whites

On December 30, 1986, at about 5 p.m. I was at the head of a party on what was supposed to be a trail. I turned 360 degrees and the woods all looked the same. It was dark. We had been up New Hampshire's 5,700-foot Mount Jefferson for the last ten hours and were trying to get down. We were "benighted." Not just in the dumb sense of the word, but we were actually caught out after nightfall, away from camp and a long way from anything else.

I was tired. I wasn't cold because walking on snowshoes and climbing icy boulders with crampons is hot, sweaty work. I had eaten gumdrops, raisins, chocolate chips, and peanuts all day to keep my internal fires burning. It isn't easy to eat L-school's recommended pound of gorp a day. I was about through my second quart of water. I knew that if we stopped for more then a few minutes I would cool down quickly. We had emergency gear. I was pretty sure we could handle a bivouac if the weather didn't change, if no one fell in a crick or broke a leg.

That kind of a night out didn't appeal to me. Weather around Mount Washington is abominable; most Yetis wouldn't like it. It is literally some of the worst in the world. I imagined sitting out a sleet storm, with no tent and only two sleeping bags for six of us. I cursed our stupidity in not sticking to our calculated turnaround time. The idea that really got to me was the vision of my funeral. It was sad and sweet. My sons behaved admirably, comforting my wife all dressed in black. It seemed a little out of character for her to spend money on a special outfit even for such a solemn occasion. I wondered who would inherit my trusted MSR stove. This line of thought amused me, comforted me and scared me. I'd never had it before.

Seventeen-year-old Justin enjoyed being lost. He took the opportunity to learn trail finding. That was good for me because it slowed the pace. Later Harold, a building contractor whose hobby is running mountain trails, said, "I just thought we'd keep on going all night." Gary didn't say anything, he was still recovering. Betty, one of our instructors, seemed more impressed. Justin and Harold were in some danger of their lives and I was surprised that it had not troubled them.

I have felt the same curious surprise other times:

When the red warning light went on in our club's Cessna Skyhawk at Toronto, I took a taxicab back to Buffalo. One of my friends flew the plane home over Lake Ontario without bothering to check with a mechanic.

We were to climb 14,000-foot Harvard in Colorado within forty-eight hours of leaving Buffalo's 600-foot elevation and damned if I could talk the group into waiting to accommodate to the altitude change. We got sick. The people I travel with don't see the same risks I see. They just want to get on with the excitement. I favor enjoying things with risk, but I want a clear view of the odds before placing my bet. In Las Vegas I play blackjack and shoot craps, the games with the most favorable odds. At craps I bet the pass line and take the odds when the shooter is making his point. This is the only reasonable bet. At blackjack I follow Professor Thorp's system and count cards. I don't play poker with guys like Amarillo Slim, and I don't play keno. My money lasts longer and I have the distinction of having been asked to leave one joint for winning.

Many mountaineers could play their game longer, if they took a better look at their way of selecting risks.

Certain of us may have "the right stuff." For them taking the very first ride in a high performance fighter might be a smart move. Chuck Yeager did well at it. But if your experience has been limited to commercial flights, you better not take a Grumman X-29A for a joy ride.

Now back to L-school. It is the Leadership section of the annual Winter School run by the Adirondack and Appalachian Mountain Clubs. It is held in the shadow of Mount Washington at the "White Mountain School" outside Littleton. Section A is a basic course in winter hiking and camping held there at the same time. Section B is the next step up. It is held in the Adirondacks at Mount Marcy. We were told that the people would ask us about the things we were doing. We were advised to be understanding and helpful. It was even hinted that some of us might return in later years as leaders. We started to feel like an elite corps, like Green Berets or something.

In 1984, I withdrew from B school after the first twenty-four hours; the time devoted to checking gear. I was pleased they let me come back in

1985. That time I stayed the whole week.

In 1986 when I saw the L school schedule, it looked like a winter picnic. There was to be a half-day of talking and planning, two day-hikes and then a three-day trip. That meant only two nights out and a lot of hot catered breakfasts and dinners. There was time allotted everywhere for lectures, planning, and review. It looked as if the emphasis was to be cerebral, not physical. Looks can be deceptive.

As has become my habit, since I discovered Winter School, I said goodbye to my family on Christmas Day. I spent the night in a run-down, over-priced motel in Rutland, Vermont. The menacing of the place put me in mind of the Adirondack motel in Ian Flemming's early James Bond novel *The Spy Who Loved Me*. There was less excitement where I stayed.

On December 26, I found my way past little farms and giant ski areas to Littleton and then to the school just off Interstate 93. It is a friendly collection of white painted clapboard buildings on a big open campus.

I was greeted warmly by instructors and started moving my gear in. As I introduced myself to a student, nearby a familiar voice said "Larry Beahan — I know you." His bearded face, compact figure and that voice melded. John, the intensely helpful and controlling instructor I had described in "Winter School Dropout," came into focus. "I hear you've gone into literature," he announced.

I fumbled, "That's right. Nice to see you again, John."

The ironic sound of John's greeting stays with me like the clang of a prison door. Yet now I see something in his point of view that I missed last time. I overheard John describe someone, it might well have been himself, as the kind of mountaineer who takes his tent along to the 7-Eleven and when he goes in belays off the bumper of his car. After L-school I'd skip the belay, but bring a tent.

John was helpful, as usual. When I set up my tent on the iced-over lawn in front of the main building he was there with a hammer and spikes to replace my plastic tent stakes. He commented on the sensitivity of Moss domed tents to the placement of the poles in their sleeves, as he noticed but didn't mention the misplacement of mine. I took his hint. The tent went up better. But I stood my ground and didn't let him put it up.

He got me again on the second day as we were going up Mount Lafayette. Old John was giving his lecture on having a prize for the kid who showed him the first "hot spot" from chafing boots and a better prize for the third one. Damn! If I didn't get first prize.

The school sent us ninety pages of material on leadership, mountaineering and first aid, useful, enjoyable stuff. I wish there had been time to

Mt. Lafayette

talk those articles out.

An excerpt from the writings of that masterful clothing salesman Yvon Chouinard impressed me. He said you might be safer if you travel with minimal equipment and rely on speed and agility to stay out of danger. His attitude sounds like test pilot stuff, but it has real appeal when you are carrying a 65-pound pack.

I found at L-school that there were differences among experienced mountaineers. There was a second instructor named John. I'll call him Jack here and apologize to him later. He is average height or less, has the build of a wrestler or gorilla and often looks as if he is about to be sick over his cud of tobacco. (Maybe I'd better apologize now. But he doesn't need the tobacco to prove his competence.)

Jack travels light. On the lower reaches of Jefferson he was dressed in Koflach boots, a pack, and a red union suit, period. For our three-day trip he came without a stove and brought only gorp for food. Betty, his partner, had left the menu planning to him and seemed a little disappointed.

Jack checked my equipment, but not like John's fine-tooth combing. Sharon called out the items. I showed some of them to Jack. I told him about others. I even got away with telling him it was too tough to stuff and unstuff my sleeping bag. John would have been on me, measuring the bag with calipers. They didn't have to worry. I was *Ready*.

Starting to climb Mount Jefferson, we students immediately went off on a wrong trail. I came back and asked if it was OK to continue over the ridge after the (fictitious) moose we were following. Jack said, "Yes, but you may have to eat moose steak for dinner." On the trail he let us make our own "moose steaks," showed us bear claw marks on trees and deer-nibbled brush and found our way off Jefferson when we were lost.

Of course the group John went with never got lost at all. They also never got to the top of the mountain. When we dragged ourselves back to camp there was John, worrying about how to rescue us if we didn't show.

The way Jack got us out of the bush is worth commenting on. We tried preserving our night vision by not using lights, but no one could see any trail. Jack had a good strong headlamp. With it he found limbs and fallen logs that had been cut by a saw or machete rather than broken. They were rare enough that they took some finding. We were then on the Link Trail between the Israel Ridge Path and Castle Ravine Trail. (I believe in low-impact camping, but whoever maintains that trail is overdoing it.)

Betty is a virologist who runs marathons and has an invitation to climb Everest. Her style is closer to Jack's. She leads and teaches with example and enthusiasm. "These crampons feel so powerful," she'd say as she strode up a near vertical sheet of wind-packed snow. Or, "Hey that's a smart idea chopping steps with your ice axe." I wish I had been a little smarter. I would have refitted my Sherpa Lightfoot snowshoes with Tucker Claw crampons, the way the equipment list suggested. Then I would not have needed to cut steps.

When we were coasting down the summit cone of Jefferson, enjoying the view of Mount Adams across the clouds, I let out a triumphant whoop and she said, " Yeah—now you're getting it." I was glad she noticed I was enjoying myself, but I think she was mistaken about me. I already knew that feeling of accomplishment. I was not converted to a new point of view. I had just been arguing that we go after that feeling in a more relaxed way.

Others seemed too dead set on achieving the next goal. They wanted to get to the top of whatever bump we were on or complete the class schedule as planned or get to a pre-picked campsite. I wanted enough time to plan what we were to do, do as much of it as was convenient, come back and talk about it and get enough rest to have fun with the next challenge.

Lee was the school leader. He handled the logistics well and set a friendly, orderly tone. I enjoyed the silly game with which he started us off. We stood outdoors in a circle and threw a ball to whoever's name we knew, calling out the name. It's a good way to learn names. We were supposed to do this on snowshoes but it didn't work out that way.

At graduation Lee even came up with diplomas for us. They were emblazoned with the school motto, "If your feet are cold put your boots on." (Which is a take-off on the old saw, "If your feet are cold put your hat on.")

On the third day, when we came back exhausted from the trip up Lafayette, I suggested that a day of rest would be welcome. I had doubts that Lee would change the schedule, but I got some support from other students so I pushed it. He finally offered a compromise. We would start the three-day trip two hours later and use a shorter approach route to the base camp. I was also given the option of not going. I think I overdid it. I pushed myself out on a limb. I didn't want to saw it off. I did want to speak out for myself and for the others who looked tired but said little. So I bought the deal. Everyone else was pleased with the extra rest, especially Betty who had a dandy cold.

I might not have given in so easily if I had not been rattled. I took it to heart when they told us to keep well hydrated. Identifying with the instructors I brought a Nalgene bottle full of water to the meeting so I could keep drinking. Following another suggestion I had dedicated one bottle the night before to answer natures needs, without leaving my tent. In the heat of the discussion I couldn't be sure I had the right bottle.

Lee did compromise but his attitude was—keep to the schedule, complete the curriculum, get to the top of the mountain, don't worry about discomfort. Discomfort can be translated, danger, in less careful hands.

There is too much "Come back with your shield or on it" attitude among mountaineers. Some lip service is paid to its opposite "Safety first." This Spartan attitude is probably what killed those fourteen kids on Mount Hood in 1986.

I even find a degree of compulsive heroism in John. On the hike to the base camp on Jefferson I had to do a lot of persuading to get our group to stop in time to make camp before dark. Harold and Justin wanted to get to where we had said we were going.

When we were set up I bet Harold that John and his group would not pass us. I assumed that John would certainly make camp in daylight. As we were eating our freeze-dried lasagna there they came. John and his group would have hiked right past us into the dusk if I hadn't yelled to them in order to save my bet.

When I got home my wife persuaded me to watch some television. The inducement was the story of the first ascent of Nanga Parma. The climb was by an Austrian-German team in 1953. They saw it as a chance to redeem their tarnished national honor.

The tension in the story developed between the conservative, authoritarian leader and a gifted, self-willed young hero. Their attempt would have failed if the kid had not defied orders and made for the summit on his own. To make it tougher he was having hallucinations and suffering from high altitude pulmonary edema. The poor guy lucked out and came home with his name in the record book. Twenty-seven people climbed K2 in 1986 and thirteen died trying. These are our heroes.

I believe that everyone in mountaineering identifies with these heroes. I think a lot of that identification is unconscious. Our admiration of them and wish to be like them is there but we are not aware of the strength and the depth of it. Consciously we say, "Me? On Everest? Without oxygen? Never happen." Yet in the back of our minds or unconsciously, we are all Walter Mittys struggling up that rock face with the Sherpas.

It is this identification that leads us to press on regardless, to ignore the turnaround time, to go out even if we are bone tired and sick. Such powerful motivation can be useful if you are a Chuck Yeager or a Horatio-at-the-bridge. I think we often push ourselves too hard and take too much risk because we unconsciously expect the good luck and rewards of heroes.

If mountaineers could get this attitude out in the open we could make better decisions about risk taking. Sometimes we might decide to try the outer limits of the "envelope." But we would weigh the risk and knowingly pick the job of "test pilot." Or we might prefer the safety and comfort of "flying commercial."

L-school would be better with more time to talk and plan and rest, but it was marvelous. My thanks to our generous and talented instructors Lee, Betty, Jack, and Sharon, and especially to John. Thanks also to my fellow students Gary, Harold, and Justin for putting up with me.

AFTERTHOUGHTS

Plastic double boots like the Koflachs are probably the best solution for winter camping. They are light, warm, waterproof, flexible at the ankle and rigid where the crampons go. Neither my randonet skiboots nor my black "mouse" boots have all these qualities.

The Zarsky Sac is a great idea. It is a huge, lightweight wind proof bag. If you crowd six people into it you are going to get warm no matter what.

Give up the idea of trying to remember where true north and magnetic north are. Forget about "East is least." Just draw magnetic north lines on your maps before you go out and stick to magnetic headings.

If you are going to gain much altitude, don't fill your fuel bottles tight. My fuel expanded and leaked.

At the school we were told that a 20-to 25-pound pack added little or no

Mt. Lafayette

physiologic burden in climbing. That's about what we carried on our summit trips and from that experience I'd agree. I also have to agree that in the first aid exercise on the final day I should have taken off my 65-pound, sofa-sized pack before tending to poor Harold. I guess I hoped we'd get Harold better quick so we could get back to school and talk it over.

Saint Regis Solo

"I vant to be alone." Garbo said it well. Last August I got that feeling. I hadn't been in the woods for awhile. Work was getting to be a chore. On the spur of the moment, I said, "The heck with all you civilized people. I'm out'a here."

I picked up a copy of *Adirondack Canoe Waters North Flow* by Paul Jamieson and Donald Morris and headed for the Saint Regis Canoe Area north of Saranac Lake.

Since I would be alone I prepared carefully. I would not be able to rely on someone else to remember the matches or extra batteries. I tested my gasoline stove. I practiced balancing my 30-pound canoe on top of the extension bar on my pack frame. I bought fresh bagels and Chinese noodle soup and was off, *All by myself.*

There was no one I had to talk to or with whom to compromise. If I wanted to stop for a cinnamon bun in Harrisville, I needed only consult myself. What bliss.

At 5:30 Thursday afternoon I drove through the meticulously groomed golf course where once stood the renowned Saranac Inn. The billiard-table-smooth greens and the little putt-putt golf carts seemed disquietingly near to my wilderness retreat. Still, I was grateful that the club allowed access to the canoe take-out on Hoel Pond.

My trip would end there so, taking Mr. Jamieson's advice, I looked it over. This should, indeed, make it easier to find from the water on my return, I thought.

A young couple was just loading into their canoe. I was tempted to speak to them. I wondered, isn't it a little soon for me to come out of isolation? I haven't even started paddling.

It dawned on me that I was reluctant to ask them for advice. This trip was to be a trial or middle-aged quest, not just a search for solitude. The question was, could I do this thing on my own?

Middle-aged isn't even fair since so few of us reach a hundred-and-twenty, I observed to myself.

Common sense got the better of me and I said, "Hello."

The young man said, "Hi, we're camped over on Turtle Pond. Just popped over for a bite to eat. Where you headed?"

I told them, "I'm going to do the nine carries route." And then I asked,

"Do you think I can get across Little Clear Pond and into Saint Regis in time to set up camp tonight?"

"Sure, no problem. You can probably get across the lake in fifteen minutes and the carry isn't very long."

"Are you going alone?" the girl asked.

"Yep," I replied. "Got three days."

"Oh boy, aren't you lucky," she said.

Although I had been telling myself I wanted to be alone, I found that conversation quite enjoyable.

At the Little Clear Pond parking lot I started thinking, gee, I'd like something good to eat before I start on freeze-dried rations. Hearing no argument, I went to a little pizza and submarine shop. It's all there is for miles around. They served me a delicious steak submarine slathered with sauce and dripping molten mozzarella. I reasoned curiously, forget the cholesterol. If I don't survive this trip, I'll regret missing this great eating opportunity.

It was getting on toward dusk when I got back to Little Clear. I admitted that I was procrastinating. Perhaps I did have some reluctance about doing this thing alone. I loaded the canoe and pressed on across the pond, anyway.

The distinction between a lake and a pond is not well defined in the Adirondacks. Little Clear Pond is no duck pond. I had a good mile and a half of paddling. The portage at the other end was not at all obvious. The map showed it a short way into the swampy shallows that surround the outlet. I paddled back and forth and in and out of those reeds quite awhile. I almost began to wish there were another set of eyes along to help.

It was getting dark when I finally made out the portage sign. I thought, should I go back to the car, camp here or make the carry over to Saint Regis Pond? It's illegal to camp on Little Clear. I remember the time the airplane spotted Teck and me camped illegally down in Allegany. What a pain that was, getting rousted at midnight. "Ahh, let's go for it," I muttered.

When I got over to Saint Regis Pond it was dark. Shadowy outlines of trees showed me where the shoreline lay. The sky was overcast so I got no help from the moon. Yet, I found I could see better without my headlamp. The map had indicated three campsites a short distance ahead on the right, out of the buggy swamp where I had arrived.

I paddled carefully in that direction. Soon I thought I saw a slight thinning of trees against the sky. I felt my way ashore. Son of a gun, it was

Fog clearing Long Pond.

a campsite. I set up my tent and hung my bear bag none too skillfully. Then, instead of enjoying the dark lonely wilderness, I opened a facsimile of civilization in the form of *The Atlantic Monthly* and read by candlelight. As I did so, I ignored, with some effort, the critter that rattled around in my canoe.

It was overcast again in the morning. Looks like rain, I thought. The pond was smooth except for one awkward loon who paddled and flapped between water and air for an incredibly long straight streak before giving up the project. It took me awhile to take off last night too but I did better than that, I laughed at him.

This is it, I thought, "Free at last." Here I am all alone on a wilderness lake. Smell that air. Look at those rock islands and the cliffs and all those bays. What a backdrop the mountains make, covered with virgin white pines. "Yeah, let's take a closer look," I said and paddled off into the picture.

As I circumnavigated Saint Regis Pond, I took the trouble to chat with nine different parties. Not too much chance of getting lonesome or lost in this wilderness, I thought. The guidebook says since the state took over it's a lot better. It used to be lined with permanent tent-camps and full of outboard motorboats.

At the three-quarter mile carry into Ochre Pond, I spoke briefly to another young couple. They passed me as I made my well-burdened single carry. At the other side, they went back for their second load. I was long-gone before they returned.

On Mud Pond, to avoid the bugs, I ate lunch afloat. There were some bugs on the trip but I don't recall one actual bite. I use various lines of defense, DEET, long sleeves and a little battery-driven buzzer. I wear the buzzer around my neck. I've painted eyes on it to add totemic force.

Fish Pond was virtually deserted when I got there early Friday afternoon. The hefty portage into it keeps the traffic down, I suppose.

I took possession of Blagden lean-to on its north shore. The lean-to on the south shore is in a state of some disrepair and has a mud floor. It did have a nice supply of split wood, though.

I mused, I certainly don't miss the weight of an axe up here, but that wood looks tempting. I'll take some and pay it back sometime, somewhere.

Back at Blagden, as I was about to unload the "borrowed" firewood I noticed a large frog staring accusingly at me from the shore two feet away. I stared back. Then I addressed him, "So how is it with you today, sir?" Silence. "This isn't your firewood is it?" The poor blighter didn't say a word. He just leaped straight at the side of my canoe, banged his head and disappeared.

While I prepared dinner, a chipmunk made a pass at my foodbag. He zoomed through camp so quickly we had no time for talk.

I went down to the shore to filter some water for soup. I watched the sun going down. Two coyotes or owls or something started howling back and forth from one shore to the other. So I joined in. I think they believed my howls. One of them gave up. The other answered me several times.

Here I am, supposedly enjoying being alone and I'm so accustomed to conversation that I'm inventing it, or am I? I've always enjoyed talking to dogs, cats, and horses, why not chipmunks, frogs, and coyotes?

Then I remembered the chipmunk and my exposed dinner. I must have scared him off with my cold stare when he breezed past earlier. Or maybe that dizzy frog warned him about me. My foodbag was not disturbed.

That night the split wood let me read by firelight. When it ran out, I retired to the double security of my little tube tent set up inside the lean-to. I was well-defended against bugs and rain. Neither materialized.

Saturday was to be the peak of the adventure. I rose early primed to explore the most interior lakes of the Saint Regis area, Little Fish Pond, and Little Long Pond.

High ridges divide these ponds from each other. The geological term for such a ridge is esker. They were formed by sediment from glacial rivers. A short steep climb up one side and down the other takes you from pond to pond. They are treacherous when wet, but fascinating.

I walked the esker between Little Fish and Little Long enjoying the spectacle of the two lakes so dramatically divided. I sought out the kettle hole described by Jamieson and Morris. A late melting ice chunk off the last glacier left this circular crater fifty feet deep and fifty yards across. As I stood in its center I thought, what a perfect fairy glen, all carpeted with soft green ferns. I prepared for Leprechauns, pipers, and a jig which, despite my state of isolation, did not appear.

That was the day's fun. What came next was much schlepping. I made the three-quarter mile carry into Clamshell Pond, paddled across and decided to take a break before taking on the next mile of portage. I hauled out *The Atlantic* and read another short story. This one was right up my alley, about Grey Owl, the Englishman who came to Canada, thought he was an Indian and convinced everyone, including the king, that he was. He used to talk to beavers, too. He's my kind of guy, I thought. Then I took a nap.

Two intruders, fishermen who had left their canoe back at Turtle Pond, my next destination, awakened me. "Be careful, the trail is awful steep and slippery," the one with the moustache said. "You sure you want to go back that way?"

"The snooze was supposed to get me ready for it," I said jauntily as I struggled to get my canoe up on top of my pack frame.

"Do you want help?" he asked.

Assuming he just meant help getting loaded up and that he was not offering to carry my canoe to Turtle Pond, I decided to go for the image of self-reliance. "No thanks, this may look awkward but it works."

I left, going uphill and around a bend. All of a sudden the trail disappeared. What in the dickens? I thought.

An elderly giant of a maple had fallen. Its roots, trunk and spreading branches made a formidable obstacle, particularly if you're carrying a canoe and full pack. There were a few more of these troublesome behemoths on the way, but I negotiated them.

I began to feel good about my portaging capacity. Let's show off a little and take some pictures of this trail wreckage while I'm carrying the canoe, I thought. So I tried a few shots, carefully catching the bow of my inverted canoe extended out overhead.

Being able to accomplish this was satisfying. The fishermen's trepi-

College kids and my one-way portage system.

dation about it turned it into conquest.

So I arrived at Turtle Pond having completed the nine carries. I could make it out to the car today but it's only Saturday, I debated. Nah, let's tack Little Long Pond on to the end of this trip. The decision was reached by acclaim.

Long Pond can be reached without portaging and this was a prime summer weekend. There were plenty of people on the pond, but still it's big enough so you don't feel crowded. I was lucky to find a campsite, especially one with a nice big lump of granite to sit on and soak up the sun.

In the evening I went for a paddle down the southern fork of the pond. I admired the few clouds at its western end. They were vividly backlighted by the setting sun that gave them a shimmering lining of silver.

The water was still. As I changed direction, coming around a point of land and out from a shadow, I was suddenly disoriented. It felt as if my canoe had been heeled far to one side. I almost capsized in an automatic attempt to right it. The clouds were so perfectly and unsuspectedly reflected in the water that it seemed the sky was abruptly where the water had been. In an instant I recognized the illusion. I was delighted that I had been so completely fooled and relished the vivid image in the water.

Then my eye was drawn to the eastern end of the pond where the yellow light of the low-angled sun turned the green of the forest to yellow and emerald. The small cedars on the shore took on an unreal quality. They looked so neatly trimmed I thought the Leprechauns were at it again.

The night was clear, starry, and cold. I woke to find that the cold air over the warm pond had produced a dense fog. From my tent, I could see nothing beyond the shoreline, absolutely nothing. I'll never find the portage in this, I thought.

Then an apparition came flying out of the gray bank a few yards away. No, not Grey Owl, it was a sweating, panting canoe marathoner with headband and slender Kevlar canoe. He charged past, bent on his morning workout, visibility or no.

I still couldn't see the other shore when I started out, compass dangling around my neck. I got only a short distance when I made out the silhouette of a loon. I changed direction a little and paddled silently toward him. I was pleased that he let me come close to him. I could make out his black head, long pointed beak, and white back markings. Then he preened, stood up in the water and dove. He came up several yards ahead, but still visible through the fog. I stalked him again. Again as I glided close he dove. We repeated the game several times until I noticed the portage sign. His next dive took him away. I called after him, "Thanks, Loon baby but I gotta' go now."

OK, you don't have to believe me but when I didn't follow, he hooted back at me. By golly, seeing-eye loons, ain't that something else?

As I approached the golf course landing on Hoel Pond I gloated. I pulled it off, a tour of Saint Regis without the help of another human hand, well, excluding Jamieson and the cartographers and a few others.

Walking unencumbered the three miles back to my car at Little Clear Pond was a delight. It was a sunny Sunday morning. I felt independent; self-confident and vastly superior to all those golf dudes riding around in little carts.

As I approached my car I was pleased with myself for not having lost my car key. I unlocked the door, got in and luxuriated in the familiar comfort.

I turned the key in the ignition and nothing happened. I muttered, "Oh nuts," or something to that effect. Suddenly, the limits of autonomy and independence became clearer. I thought, I don't "vant to be alone." I vant to find someone who can give me a jump-start.

A nice young guy with a pick-up truck got me out of that fix.

Sometimes I get very hungry for the experience of being alone in the woods. Soon after I'm there, I crave people and home again. I take pleasure in the going and coming. Like changing seasons, like life and death, awareness of the one enhances the other.

Garbo is gone and all alone now. As I test my competence alone in the woods and perhaps foolishly court disaster, I show myself that my own final aloneness is a little way off yet. There is immense pleasure in that process of looking and in that discovery.

Reflections or an underworld?

Doug instructing.

White Water, Green Paddler

What is that marvelous smell? Mmmmm, it's fresh brewed coffee. I am just waking up.

I fell out of my cot last night. It has a severe list to port. Lyn and I have a small room at the end of the hall. Outside our door there is a hole in the floor that used to be the system for heating the upstairs. Just beneath it stands the coffee machine which is cheerily available twenty-four hours a day, but smells so especially good early in the morning.

Downstairs in the kitchen we hear rattlings and rumblings. Sue and Doug have been up for awhile. The crew is gathering at the long plank picnic benches in the dining room and are addressing huge platters of French toast and bacon. Lyn and I decide to scoop into the big bucket of steaming oatmeal and douse it with cinnamon sugar for starters.

It is early in the season, April 21, and a cold weekend is forecast. There is not a big crowd for breakfast here at W.I.L.D.W.A.T.E.R.S. Glen House in Warrensburg on the upper Hudson River. But they are hungry, enthusiastic and rugged looking. Beards and woolen shirts are prevalent. The talk is of this river and that rapids and, "What are you going to do today?"

Glen House is unprepossessing from the outside. It is a big old clapboard farmhouse with an enclosed porch wrapped around it. But it sits just across the road from an excellent patch of white water in the Hudson River and it is not far from several other spectacular runs.

The porch doubles as mud room and retail shop for the lodge. It is stocked with dry suits, PFD's, paddles and other paraphernalia of the trade. The living room is the next thing you see. A nice big fire in the brick fireplace usually dominates it. There are well-used overstuffed chairs and a big comfortable couch. Hobo and Topaz, the cats, can usually be persuaded to share the couch if you provide a little gentle stroking. Prominent among the magazines strewn about are *Canoeing* and *Adirondac*. In one corner there is a large TV with a VCR. The tapes did not look real interesting. They included *Friday the Thirteenth III*, *My Bloody Valentine* and *Revenge of the Nerds*. Later in the weekend we did some watching and *The Nerds* wasn't that bad, particularly in contrast to the videos of me in my canoe trying to do a "Cross Dufek." We spent some good time chatting in front of that fire.

When we arrived Friday afternoon we were greeted by a big, friendly, furry sheep dog and then by a guy looking kind of weird in his wet suit and helmet, and with a kayak over his shoulder. He told us the others were probably out on a trip and would be back soon.

Doug Azaert runs his W.I.L.D.W.A.T.E.R.S. canoeing, kayaking, and rafting operation from Glen House and it is ideal for the purpose. Room and board is inexpensive and the location is perfect.

Then it was Saturday morning after breakfast.

I came up here to the wild upper reaches of the Hudson River to polish my white water paddling technique. What am I doing in this shallow cove off Loon Lake? There is snow in the air. The wind is blowing like crazy. My feet are numb. It is chilly and damp inside my wet suit. I reach over the side of my new Blue Hole, Sunburst canoe (They had asked why it wasn't very scratched up. I explained that I was very careful.) and I execute a flawless draw stroke. There is a gust of wind. Oops! I'm sitting in eighteen inches of water and six of mud. It is much colder inside my wet suit. I'm glad I'm not tumbling in the Hudson's rapids.

Most of my canoeing has been on flat water. Once you get the hang of doing a "J" stroke or just switching sides it is not hard to get from one place to another. Last year I bought a white water canoe to make it a little more exciting. I read a book on white-water. I went on two white water trips with our Niagara Frontier Chapter. Both were near Buffalo, one on the Cattaraugus, the other on the Genesee. They were said to have class two and three rapids. I did a little eddying in and eddying out, some ferrying and some surfing. I got through them OK.

But Doug has some different ideas about paddling in white water. He looks really good at it and has an excellent reputation so I was eager to learn but "It ain't easy."

First of all you are supposed to discipline yourself to paddle primarily on one side and always keep the same hand at the top of the paddle no matter which side you are on. This means that you have to learn twice as many strokes as you would if allowed to change hands. You learn to sweep, draw, scull, power, and Dufek and then you learn their cross-counterparts which can twist you out of shape considerably.

I tried talking Doug out of this with the story of, I think it was Spartacus the galley slave who became a gladiator. He persuaded the authorities to let him row a little on each side of the ship in order to develop himself evenly. This cut no ice with Doug. He said you need the one-sided technique for speed and agility when maneuvering in white water and that all really good C-1 ers came out lopsided.

These strokes are executed with the power in them coming mainly from the rotation of your torso rather than from your arms. The power strokes are amazingly short and choppy but when done right can make the boat literally jump forward. The "Dufek" is a forward rudder named after a Czech canoeist that defected to the west. It amuses me to think that my defective Dufek is named after Dufek the defector.

Being securely braced in your canoe, with thigh straps, helps immensely with transferring the force of your strokes to the boat and in leaning the boat. By leaning it is possible to take advantage of the curving waterline of your boat to turn it, much like the curving edge of a ski turns you on snow.

Having a paddle of appropriate length is very important in executing strokes in the proper vertical manner.

Doug retied my thigh straps and loaned me a longer paddle. After I capsized I arranged to buy a dry suit from him which proved much more comfortable than my wet suit in those temperatures

After the capsize, they complimented me on my picturesque but ineffective "air brace." Then we went into the techniques of high and low braces. In these maneuvers you very abruptly slap the full length of your paddle flat on the water, rather like a beaver warning his family. This produces a powerful righting force and can save you a dunking.

We returned to the Glen for dry clothes and very welcome buckets of hot soup and piles of grilled cheese sandwiches washed down with hot chocolate. Doug's younger brother Tony had dumped earlier and got wetter and colder than I did so he and Ira signed off for the afternoon. Ira and Tony are kind of instructors-in-training and general roustabouts. Part of their benefits are instructions. Mike Haley is the chief rafting guide. The three of them had joined us in the morning. I had signed up for a weekend of group lessons but with the weather, I turned out to be the only paying student. It was rather nice having that much special attention. They really did make me feel a part of the family.

The camaraderie and spirit among them, including Sue who guides, cooks and administers, struck me. They have devoted themselves full time to something they love and are good at. They are at the cutting edge of something difficult, exciting, and fun. They know all the champions. They are out of the rat race and doing what they want to. I envy that, but don't, just, have the courage to do it myself.

Saturday afternoon we did some more work on strokes at Loon Lake. Lyn went off and climbed Hackensack Mountain back of Warrensburg. In the morning she had come along to take pictures. She doesn't really believe in canoeing, especially when it is snowing out.

At dinner Sue had two kinds of pasta, one with traditional red sauce, the other mixed with vegetables and a cheese sauce, plenty of carbohydrates for cold hungry paddlers. The talk after dinner was of the rescue in the gorge of the Hudson. A party had gone in with a keg of beer instead of a guide and without proper clothing. The bottom got torn out of their raft and they were very, very cold by the time the rangers led them out. The other big item was a proposal by a local company to operate an eighty-acre gravel pit that would run a steady stream of trucks along the River Road through the Glen. The DEC was to hold a hearing, and a petition to oppose the project was circulated.

On Sunday, a crew of twenty-five rafters came in. Ann and the boys provided them a wild, cold, ride in the Hudson while Mike and Doug and I went after some white water in the Schroon River. We played in the rapids staying just below them and practiced ferrying, peeling in and out of eddies, and surfing. I tried using the new strokes but not with very great success. Finally I said "the heck with it" and started using my old catch-as-catch-can technique. I could get around, though rather inexactly, in the white water and it was fun. Doug looked on a bit exasperated. He had put a lot of effort into teaching me the day before and I was a very small class. So I tried it some more his way.

In the afternoon we were down to Doug and me alone. We went back to the flat water and I think I did make some progress in mastering American Canoe Association white water technique.

Lyn and I had a delightful weekend at W.I.L.D.W.A.T.E.R.S.

Loosening up for paddling.

Bearhunter and Me

Walking the road-like trail to Lake Lila in the Nehasane preserve, I found myself in the company of a stranger. I'll call him "Bearhunter."

As I overtook Bearhunter he had an incongruous look about him. He worried along behind him a thing that resembled a shopping cart. He'd stop and swear at it now and again. As I got closer I could see the thing he was pulling was a tiny canoe mounted on wheels. Contained in this vehicle was a shopper's list of what my sometimes too critical eye saw as disreputable camping gear. So I'm a snob, but I still don't approve of his egg-crate-open-cell foam-rubber mattress.

He was in need of a shave. He wore camouflage coveralls and he talked incessantly. Over his shoulder he carried a worn, bolt-action, thirty-ought-seven rifle. He apologized about the rifle. "My father talked me out of bringing the good gun. I got one that's all engraved and everything. Looks a whole lot better than this one. Don't shoot any better, though."

Until then, it had been a dandy September morning. The sky was clear. It was chilly in the sunshine, so a wool shirt felt good. The leaves were just starting to turn. It was green and yellow against flashing blue water and bright sky, with once in a while a splash of maple's scarlet.

The quality of the day was the second thing Bearhunter had on his mind. Eventually he said, "Great day, huh?" But way before that, came the question, "Have you got some matches? I buried my darn matches down in the pack there somewhere." He had an unlighted cigarette hanging sadly from the corner of his mouth.

The last thing I wanted to do was breathe cigarette smoke out there. I lied and told him, "No."

I immediately felt guilty about that and it got worse because he proved so friendly and such a fountain of information. At first I was just going to dust on past him as quick as I could. He kept on talking so I wasn't able to do that, without offense.

He assured me again that he had matches buried under his load somewhere. "I'd never come out here in the woods for four days without some kind of fire."

He also told me he had just turned forty and had to get away from the family and kids awhile to get used to being that old.

I kind of nodded to him sideways, trying not to trigger any more socialization. Then he dropped the fact that he was going "bear hunting."

My ears perked up at this. It reminded me that this was bear hunting season and I was out in the woods without any bright clothing to protect me from being mistaken for a bear. It also brought vividly to mind an encounter with a mother bear who had started to pursue me the previous month. Besides that, I had just come from Old Forge, where the town was alive with the controversial killing of Old Split Ear, a 685-pound black bear addicted to the town garbage dump.

I'd been browsing in the book section of that huge wonderful hardware store in Old Forge. A middle-aged saleslady collared me and lectured half an hour on the life and times of Old Split Ear. Then she sold me Stephen Herrero's excellent book, *Bear Attacks, Their Causes and Avoidance* which scared the wits out of me.

I fell into Bearhunter's pace for the three-mile walk. He had been to Lake Lila forty times, so he said. This was my first. He hunted with bow as well as rifle. He had gotten four deer with his bow over the years and seen a lot of bear while deer hunting. "I've only seen one bear while I was hunting bear, though. Never got a shot at one. If I ever killed a bear, one would be enough, I think. I wouldn't have to get any more. Them bear, they come right at you and snap their teeth like they want you to beat it. I'm not going to run this time, if they do it. I'll stand right up to them."

I was wondering what Bearhunter would do with the carcass if he shot even an average-sized 300-pound bear. He was having enough trouble pulling that cart without a bear on top of it. I also wondered if he thought I was being impolite by not offering him a hand with the cart. I prepared myself to argue the point, but he was considerate enough not to raise it. I finally managed to break into his rapid stream of monologue by catching him when he inhaled. "Do you hunt bear from a tree stand?" I quickly asked.

"What?" he said. He didn't hear my whole question because it had come in over some of his last statement. I got halfway through repeating my question, and he interrupted laughing. "You shoot a bear in the butt with an arrow and you better be in a tree. A bear can get pretty mad."

He went on to describe the pot of honey and molasses he planned to cook over his fire, "To give them bears some motivation." Of course he didn't stop there. He talked about his family, his hunting, he complained about the lousy wheels on his cart, about the Vermont company that has the contract for the lumber in here and only lets Vermonters drive the road we were hiking, and other things.

The old railroad station at Lake Lila.

When he took his second breath I said, "I ran into a sow and two cubs up in Algonquin Park a month ago and she took off after me." I waited, but he didn't ask me to go on. Instead he started telling me how to improve my hike here at Lake Lila. "You know, I followed these railroad tracks back of the lake. If you go back there a little ways the old railroad station house is still there. It's in great shape but the tracks, look out; they are all tore up. Lots of berry bushes in there, too. Bears love berries. Might see a bear back there. Boy, I love this weather and being out here, don't you?"

I started to say, yup, but he didn't wait that long. He pointed to a rotten log that had been smashed to bits and said, "A bear might have done that, looking for grubs." There were some overturned flat rocks; he went on, "Might have been that same bear looking for worms or whatever."

I was catching on to his rules of conversation. Answer your own questions. Don't be a sucker and ask the other guy anything that lets him get

Bear bags hanging in a giant white pine at the Lake Lila lean-to.

into one of his stories. Somehow when he wasn't paying attention I slipped in my story about the time I was sleeping in my tent at Lake Colden. A bear bumped me and woke me up as he charged past. He was going for the "bear bag" my neighbor had hung in a nearby tree. Bearhunter had stopped. He looked slyly at me saying, "You ain't supposed to do that."

"Do what?" I said.

"Hang up a bag of food for a bear. It's against the law."

I explained that they weren't baiting the bear, they were just trying to keep their food away from him by hanging it out of reach. But by then, Bearhunter was squatting down at a muddy spot in the road looking at a paw print. "Very big dog or very small bear," he said. It looked like dog to me.

I decided to let him have it with my big bear story. I said, "Couple years ago my wife and I went on a trip up to Churchill, Manitoba to look at polar bears. The guides cooked sardines on the tundra buggy's manifold to bring the bears in."

"That so?" he said. "Friend of mine and I went hunting up at James Bay and we didn't see a thing." Then he was off again. Somewhere along the way he dropped in that New York State has around four thousand black bears, second only to Pennsylvania and Maine; that eight hundred bears are harvested in our state each year; that only one in a thousand bearhunters gets a bear. He added, "Bear meat ain't bad if you boil the hell out of it with garlic, black coffee, and soda before you roast it. And be sure to put a lot of onions in with it, when you roast it, unless you like the wild taste. I do. I like that wild taste, myself."

So I had to really let him have it. "When I was up in Alaska I got some pictures of grizzlies," I said.

"I never been to Alaska," he replied. "I always wanted to go there."

I figured I had him now. I quick said, "We were visiting Denali Park and I took a joy ride in an airplane to a hunting camp where they were butchering caribou. The pilot was dropping off a guy who claimed he had killed the world record fair-chase polar bear and the skull was in that camp."

"Did you see it?" he asked, seeming to break his rule, but he was right on.

I answered, "Yes, I did," then I had nowhere to go from there. He hung on my last word. His expectant manner demanded a description of that epic chase of which I had only the barest bones. I had already given them to him. So I changed the subject. "What do you think of that Split Ear thing up at Old Forge?"

"Gee, wait till I tell my kids I met someone who's been to Alaska and takes pictures of grizzlies and polar bears," he said. I couldn't quite tell if he was mocking me out or not.

"That Split Ear was quite a big fella, 685 pounds I heard. He might have been a record," I said, shifting about uncomfortably.

"What a waste of an animal," Bearhunter said. "Did you do any hunting up there in Alaska?" he persisted.

I replied truthfully, "No."

"Ever hunt bear around here?"

"No," I answered again. "I only went hunting once in my life. That was with my dad when I was a kid. We were after woodchucks, but we didn't see anything so we shot at some tin cans."

"Tin cans," he said with some kind of questioning look. It pleased me when he dropped the subject of my exploits and finally picked up the bait on Old Forge's problem. "People were making a regular circus out of those bears in Old Forge. They closed down the dump two years ago. Twenty or thirty bears had been making a living out of that dump. Then they'd sit on their front porches, stick honey all over their feet and let Old Split Ear come and lick it off. Then someone decides Split Ear's getting to be a nuisance and they gut shoot him and let him rot in the woods. What a crying waste."

"Did you see all the letters in the *Adirondack Express* arguing about it?" I asked.

"Yes, I saw them letters and I agree with every one of them. There's two sides to every story. I can see how the guy who shot that bear was worried about his kids and ticked off about the bear waking up the dogs every night. I can see how that guy's mother would come out to back him up the way she did. After all, it was her kid. And I can see how all the people who liked to feed Split Ear got a kick out of him. I just don't see how them folks could be so stupid as to go on feeding bears in town and not realize the mess they were getting into. You feed bears and bears are going to come to your house to eat."

"I guess the Department of Environmental Conservation tried to help,"

I commented.

"Well, yes and no," he laughed. "They tried to drive Split Ear off with rubber bullets and cayenne pepper spray and air horns, but that never did any good. They even carried him away over into the Moose River Wilderness. But tell me they didn't know he'd be back. They knew that wasn't far enough. He came back next spring and got shot down like a dog. It wasn't no hunting, no sport, just murder."

By then we had reached the lake. A party with a very big dog occupied the lean-to there. I thought Bearhunter would come along with me and bend their ears too but he stood firmly on the trail. "Aren't you going to say hello?" I asked.

"Nope, I'll say good-bye here. I don't like the look of that big dog." We shook hands and parted company.

I visited at the lean-to, praised their catch of fish and patted their dog. Then I went on down the road another mile or so and found a log to sit on for lunch. I was thinking about bears and people. I thought of that poor little squirt, Bearhunter, sitting out in the woods, all alone, boiling a pot of honey and molasses. Maybe he'd attract a bear and kill it. Maybe the bear would make a meal out of Bearhunter. The odds seemed fairer out in the woods than those did that greeted poor Old Split Ear in town. Split Ear must have been so surprised when one of those nice people who left out garbage for him let him have it, in the guts, with a shotgun.

My subconscious did a funny trick then. It dragged up the image of Goldilocks marauding through the house of the three bears and of their mild reaction. "Somebody's been eating my porridge and they ate it all up." What a contrast to Old Split Ear's treatment.

Stephen Herrero's bear-attack book was fresh in my mind. Herrero says black bears are timid in comparison to grizzlies and, yet, in the U.S. and Canada between 1960 and 1980, there were five hundred black bear attacks on people. He knew of twenty-three fatalities. In 1978, three boys went fishing in Algonquin Park and were killed by a black bear. In 1990, two adults were killed by a black bear on Lake Opeongo. I wasn't far from there this summer when I met that mama bear and her two cubs picking berries. And she took offense.

Sitting there, not far from the shores of beautiful Lake Lila, peacefully eating my lunch, I heard a rustling in the brush. I took a cautious look around and saw nothing. Then there was a distinct odor of fish in the air, which I hadn't noticed before. I thought, oh, oh, bear breath. I thought I heard something more in the bushes. I picked up the remainder of my lunch and put it in my pack. I walked straight back to the road and went for home.

I don't know if there was a bear sniffing around me there at Lake Lila or if Bearhunter was trying to scare me or if it was my nerves chewing on a lot of bear data. I do know a bear didn't eat me. I didn't even see one.

I like to think, though, that it was Old Split Ear's ghost looking for a handout. But I was careful not to leave anything for him to eat, or for any of his cousins lest they get the wrong idea about the possibility of being friends with people and get themselves or some of us killed.

Skiing the Old Kunjamuk Road
(Siamese Pond Wilderness South of Indian Lake Village)

Some friends of mine were going to climb Haystack at the end of February. I was tempted to go along, but remembered how tough it had been to keep up with them on Seymour. I decided, instead, to try the luxury of a guided cross-country ski trip.

The decision was hard on my ego, but turned out to be a smart move. My friends got pinned down in heavy winds at eighteen below zero. One of them was frost bitten. While they suffered, I had a very pleasant ski through woods that I had never seen before. I met some delightful people. We carried wonderfully light daypacks and the guides did all the cooking.

I had called Walter Blount, the outfitter, on a Thursday. He said, "Sure, Andy can take care of you on tomorrow's trip." He warned me though, "Chimney Mountain Lodge can be hard to find."

Big Brook Road from Indian Lake to Kings Flow turned out to be as winding and cranky as Walter suggested. When the light began to fade, I was grateful for a set of tire tracks in the fresh snow that gave me a path to follow. The driver who made them took all the curves way to the inside, like a slalom racer whipping down poles. Finally the lodge came into view, a collection of buildings huddled at the end of the road under the massif of Chimney Mountain.

I followed the slalom course to where a truck was parked by a lighted cabin. I knocked. No one answered. I opened the door and went in past the sign saying, *"No wet boots."* I yelled, "Hello, anyone home?" There was no answer. I yelled again, "Hello, is this Adirondack Hut To Hut?"

Then an apparition appeared. He had long, bushy hair that stood out from his head all around. Tiny, round granny-glasses perched low on his nose. He was average height, but his vigorous stance made him look larger. Massive tattooed forearms extended from the sleeves of his khaki Wallace Beery shirt. Powerful legs, encased in madras shorts, supported him.

"What do you want?" he asked, out of breath and with a hint of accusation. I had the distinct feeling of having interrupted a mandatory weight-training session.

"I...ahh...made arrangements, with a fellow...named Walter...at the last minute, to...ahh...join this trip. ...Is this Adirondack Hut To Hut?" I asked again, lamely.

The apparition inhaled deeply and responded, "Yeah, this is the place, but we weren't expecting anyone before seven!"

I explained to the apparition that, since Walter said it might be hard to find, I had used daylight to get there. I told him, "Now that I've found you, I'll drive back out and get something to eat at Indian Lake and come back later." I thought he might try to talk me out of that one-mile round trip in the dark and the snow. As I left I added, "It's snowing pretty hard. I heard we were going to get five inches."

He said, "Naah, we won't get that much."

When I got back two and a half hours later, an affable guide named Andy and his portly sidekick, Bill, greeted me. There was no sign of the apparition.

Andy was cordial, reserved, and polite. Bill was flushed, jovial, and full of talk. He sells bicycles all week and was eager to get into the woods for the weekend. Andy works full time year round as a guide.

Two Kentuckians, Marlene and her daughter, Kathy, came in out of what had now become a considerable snowstorm. Marlene let it slip that, this being leap year, tomorrow, February 29, was Kathy's sixth birthday.

The phone rang and Bill announced, "Listen to this. These two girls are just now leaving New York City. They say they'll get here about 2:30 in the morning."

"Four-thirty is more like it," groaned Andy. "Who's going to let them in?"

"They might as well stay up all night," Bill laughed. "Let's just leave 'em a note and leave the light on."

Bill and Andy had a lot of catching up to do. They had taken the guide exam together. They talked of trying to persuade Walter into various deals, Bill's bike business and then, endlessly, of white water, rock climbing, skiing, and camping.

It wasn't till I had seen Andy, with his fuzzy hair standing out straight, again, working ferociously at producing a great mound of broccoli omelets, pork sausage, toast, and jam, and after my second cup of coffee, that I realized who he was. Andy was the apparition that had scared me away the night before.

He seemed in some transitional phase of being, especially when he got on me about the huge pack I wanted him to transport for me. After breakfast, when his hair was tied back in a knot and we had compromised on my pack, he shifted gears down to his quiet host persona.

There were nine of us. The girls from New York City, Pam and Joan, had stumbled into the main lodge in the wee hours. A young couple, Anne and Dan, found their way, unannounced, into one of the cabins that had been closed for the winter. Bill discovered them there, huddled in sleeping bags in the morning. The latecomers were bleary-eyed, but gung ho for the trail.

After we had eaten, Andy and Bill laid out the plan. Andy would haul our sleeping bags and as little other gear as he could talk us into by truck and snowmobile thirty miles via the town of Speculator to Cisco Brook Camp. Bill would lead us skiing ten miles across the Siamese Pond Wilderness mostly on the Old Kunjamuk Stagecoach Road to meet Andy at Cisco Brook for the night.

I had brought my compass and some emergency gear. But I didn't bring a map or even look very carefully at one. I had planned to relax in the lap of luxury and let the guides find the way. At the last minute I felt uneasy and bought Andy's last map, his "demonstrator." He gave me a dollar off.

It was two below that morning. The wind was blowing hard across Kings Flow. We were glad that it was at our backs as we stepped into skis and started single file out onto the frozen brilliant white plain that the lake presented. The sky was clear and bright. We left Chimney Mountain, the lodge and civilization behind.

Bill charged out ahead, breaking a trail in the eight inches of fresh snow that had fallen during the night. "Best snow we've had all year," he proclaimed. He was dressed in a bright blue and orange Gore-Tex ski suit and carried a mountaineering pack with a spare ski-pole tip and basket extending above it. Andy waved us on our way as he loaded gear into the truck. He wore a rough wool shirt and wool pants held up by suspenders and a big leather belt.

We had a great day of skiing over ponds, through tall stands of white pine, some uphill and a bit of pleasant down, mostly on the Old Kunjamuk Road. The trail was well maintained and easy. There were one or two recent blow-downs to circumvent. At one spot, we had to walk a narrow log across twenty feet of deep flowing water. A missed step could have been very troublesome.

Just before Pete's Hill, we stopped for lunch along Wakely Brook. It was five degrees by someone's little pull-tab thermometer. Standing still, we were getting cold fast. I pulled my down parka out of my pack and sat upon my closed cell "sit upon" to munch peanut butter and jelly and candy bars. I had finished the one water bottle I carried inside my shirt. The one in my pack had the top frozen on solid. I put it inside the parka with me until the screw top melted loose. Under the top, there was still a dome of ice I had to chop through to get at the water. We did not stay long, but we did have a little conversation.

I mentioned being on a trip once where guides came in by helicopter to cook steaks for lunch. It was only a slight exaggeration. Joan, one of the New York girls, said she'd been on one where the guides brought out instruments to provide chamber music at lunch. Later she admitted it was a lie. Bill apologized for the lack of customary amenities, but he offered to share the last of his M&Ms and whistle "Dixie" in honor of our guests from Kentucky, if that would please us.

The only difficulty we had was missing the trail exiting one of the lakes. We had to double back across the lake into the wind. This added a mile to the trek but it put us one up on Bill, who was leading the way.

Kathy remembered getting lost leading a group of teen-agers on a summer hike. She was something of a guide herself. Her campers started taunting her with a chant they invented:

Fish heads, fish heads,
Roly, poly fish heads.
Yumm!

So she and some of the others started to give Bill the roly, poly fish-heads treatment. He took it good-naturedly.

Bill was portly for a guide, but he proved to be in better shape than he looked. He broke trail for us most of the day. The pack he carried, filled with emergency supplies, was the biggest in the group and he got us where we were going. He put me in mind of another vigorous, portly outdoorsman, Teddy Roosevelt.

In 1901, Roosevelt took a wild, midnight buckboard ride down the stagecoach road from Newcomb to North Creek, not far from our Kunjamuk Road. He had been climbing Mount Marcy when the news reached him that McKinley had been shot in Buffalo. He rushed there, found him dead, and was sworn in as president of the United States.

Cisco Brook Camp is about sixty years old and was built to house a lumber crew. It stands on International Paper land on the Old Kunjamuk Road. A five-foot-tall stone nearby marks the stagecoach route.

The camp is constructed of ten-inch logs. Its hipped roof, covered with snow, gradually grew long icicle daggers during our stay. There was plenty of space inside with several doublewide bunk beds on one end and a kitchen on the other. In the center was a four-by-eight-foot boiler that had been converted into a stove. Andy claimed he put forty-one pieces of wood into that stove to get it started before we got there. It was red hot and welcome.

Guides Bill and Andy were fond of disaster stories. We heard parts of them before the trip. Bill repeated them during the ski and the two of them refined the stories that evening at Cisco Camp.

They told about Hardluck Camp up back of Round Pond. Over a short period, three successive owners had died there, one in a hunting accident, another in a truck accident, and the third of a heart attack. The State of New York now owns it. I hope we have better luck.

Somewhere between Round Pond and Cisco Brook one lumberjack, confined too long over a winter, hit his mate over the head with a U-shaped oxbow and killed him. The murderer made good his escape and it took two years to find him. He was living and working only twenty-seven miles away in North Creek.

Their favorite story was about Cisco Camp itself. When it was new, in the thirties, a lumber crew spent a winter there. A lumberjack named Freddy was a member of that crew. He had unspeakable toilet habits. These habits were so bad that Andy and Bill would not even tell us what they were. The men working and living in close quarters with Freddy found him intolerable. They cajoled, threatened and tried to persuade him to adopt more hygienic habits, but he continued blandly, unconforming. After one particularly awful episode, an infuriated lumberjack stormed out the door of the camp and shot Freddy to death as he sat in the three-holer out back. In the heat of his rage, the executioner stuffed the body through one of the holes and down into the pit. It was several years till Freddy was discovered in his grave. The feeling at the camp must have been that justice had been done for no one was ever prosecuted for the crime. Bullet holes are plainly visible in the old shed.

Before dinner, we gathered in the aged Barcaloungers and old lumpy sofas surrounding the sizzling boiler-stove. We gloated over the great skiing we had on the way out. We told stories, dried socks, and dozed, while Bill and Andy put together a Mexican fiesta for our dinner. The only help they asked was in hoisting a three-foot high, two-foot across cauldron, frozen full of ice, up on top of the boiler. Andy, Paul Bunyan-like, had dragged the behemoth into the cabin by himself and did most of the lifting onto the stove.

That evening, at the cabin's twelve-foot dining table, we ate tons of Andy's hand-rolled tacos, sour cream, refried beans, and Spanish rice. A few cans of beer turned up. Kathy's mother Marlene announced again that it was her leap-year-baby's sixth birthday and she broke out champagne. There really was not that much alcohol around, but the group was intoxicated with fatigue and the joy of escape from civilization. We were laughing, joking, and starting to get a little silly. We weren't at all prepared for the loud bang that came at the door.

The door opened with a blast of cold. A small man with a large mustache and an unplaceable accent burst in carrying a shotgun. Andy said, "Hello."

The stranger ignored him and demanded, "Have anybody seen my dog? He ees a young beagle an I teenk he runned off to be wit de coyots. Budt dey will kill heem. He's a leetle shy but eef you crouch down he will come. He knows his name, Freddy."

Freddy? Our communal eyebrows went up. Wasn't that the name of that lumberjack who died here so ignobly? Had we stepped into a bad horror movie?

Andy established where the stranger was staying, agreed that he had heard coyotes and that if we saw Freddy we would bring him down. The rest of us just watched and listened. As soon as the stranger was gone the jokes, some admittedly a little sick, started. Was this the murdered Freddy's ghost? Poor Freddy the Beagle eaten alive by his "friends" the coyotes.

Andy surprised us with a big delicious supermarket birthday cake and six candles for Kathy. The icing was in good shape. He must have balanced it in one hand as he drove the snowmobile and its trailer full of packs through the woods to camp. When we couldn't finish the cake, Dan proposed that Kathy put the remains outside so the coyotes could have dessert too, "after they're done with Freddy."

Just then there was another, this time thunderous, rap on the door. I'm not kidding, this really happened. A bigger edition of the stranger, with his own gun and mustache and accent, burst in, "I from dee nex camp. Has anybody seen dat dog name Freddy? He wander off and he don' come back. You gotta' tell eef you seen heem!"

More jokes after he left. "I told you, you shouldn't bring Freddy into the woods. I told you not to lose Freddy." This was Pam, speaking as the intruder's wife.

"The next guy will come in swinging an axe and saying, 'Where's Freddy? Why you didn't let him in the cabin to get warm?'" That was Dan.

The remarks came fast and funny. I laughed. Then I stopped and thought, what an unfunny couple of situations to laugh at— a friendly dumb pup eaten alive and a poor slob murdered?

I thought, we are all in a strange, slightly hazardous situation. It is fun, but there are risks. Maybe what we are doing is like whistling in the dark, using gallows humor. By making fun of the "fearful fate" of the Freddys I and II, we ease our own fears. Or perhaps this cruel humor amplifies our fears and puts an extra kick into the adventure.

Andy and Bill cleaned up. I sat there like nobility or a gold brick. They seemed to assume it was their job. No one argued.

We slept well and long. The next morning, for breakfast, we had stacks of Andy's famous pumpkin pancakes covered with syrup. We packed and took off, leaving him with the dishes and the packs.

I took only a quick squint at the map. We were going back a slightly different route. We would take the John Mack Trail west of Pete's Hill to Long Pond. Then we would do an easy bushwhack for a mile to pick up the Kunjamuk Road again.

The weather was a little warmer. Skiing on the trail was fast and easy. Soon we were warm and opening up jacket vents and removing hats and gloves.

As we crossed Long Pond, we got preoccupied admiring the tall gray cliffs where loons do their nesting. We pulled the same trick we had the day before; we missed the proper exit from the lake and continued down the trail into John Mack Pond. Bill was unclear on where the bushwhack began, but we found a flagged tree that seemed a likely indication and struck off there. At that point, I took a look at the map and plotted an approximate compass course for my own satisfaction.

Bill wasn't going quite the way I would have gone, but I figured he knew the way. He pointed and said confidently, "We just have to go through this valeie and out that way." Dan and Kathy nodded. I hadn't even heard the term valeie before (He pronounced it "vlay" but the closest I could come to it later in the dictionary was the Middle English term "valeie," an ancestor of valley) so who was I to question?

We came onto a beaver pond that was easy going and in the right general direction. It was fun skiing across one level, up over a dam, visiting its beaver lodge and then up over another dam onto a third level with another lodge in its middle. But then we started up into the real bush where no one may have trod for a hundred years. There were downed trees, spruce thickets, unexpected cliffs, deep snow, all manner of unpleasantries. I lost my hat, for a while, got snow down my neck and repeatedly got my skis jammed into unworkable positions.

Anne broke the tail of her ski and twisted an ankle. Dan splinted both with duct tape. Some of us worried; others clung to a "positive attitude" for security. We were getting tired. I wished I'd brought some heavy-duty skis with metal edges and maybe climbing skins instead of lightweight plastic beauties.

I started to ski down a relatively open patch. My left pole got snagged in something behind me giving my arm a nasty yank. It took that to remind me to keep my hands out of my pole loops when skiing in the woods.

I thought, what if we have gone up the wrong side of one of these hills and we are in a gully two or three over from where we thought we were? Supposing someone dislocates a shoulder and we have to backtrack to Cisco Camp with them, at this hour? It was about 2 p.m. and we had been skiing since nine.

I began to think how nice it was that some people took the pains to make trails for others. We had felt pretty adventurous whisking down a

A logger's shanty something like the one on the Kunjamuk.

trail across a "wilderness" the day before. In the middle of our bushwhack it was apparent that whisking can only be enjoyed after someone else has put in a whole lot of work building a trail. I knew Andy and his bucksaw were responsible for a lot of the easy trail skiing we had enjoyed. I wished I had spent a few minutes with him and the map before we started.

Trees and weather closed in on us so that landmarks were harder to make out. The contour map gave us an indication of what the land should look like but you couldn't see enough of the land at one time to get a good fix. I caught up to Bill, at the edge of a pond, to tell him about Anne's sprained ankle. He was studying his map and checking the compass. He said, "This has been embarrassing, but I know where we are now. This valeie looks familiar to me. We go out the northeast corner, head east and we will hit the Kunjamuk Road."

Joan said edgily, "One valeie looks a lot like another." Her statement struck me as an awful truth.

At Kathy's suggestion, we broke out food and water. Everyone took a look at the map. Bill checked Anne's ankle. She was doing all right. Then he struck out ahead and I followed while the others caught their breath.

We chewed our way through brush for twenty minutes with him way out in front. When I heard that joyous howl from him I knew he'd found it. Somewhere inside me a similar resounding yell formed, and thus the word passed down the line that we were not going to be coyote bait tonight. We were going to get home before dark.

We felt so good we took time out to stop at Round Pond for the treat of inspecting Harold's camp, a hundred-year-old two-story beauty of a log cabin. Bill claimed that on the door were bear claw scratches, made while fearful skiers huddled inside. I looked at them. I don't know. It could have been a raccoon.

Andy met us as we straggled into Chimney Mountain Lodge. Welcome snacks were strewn on the kitchen counter. We indulged in coffee, cocoa, hot showers, and dry clothes. We laughed over the slight miscalculation in navigation that had cost us two painful hours. Andy and Bill talked about their next project, Walter's twenty-kilometer race next weekend. Everyone was shaking hands and wishing each other well. "Nice skiing with you, had a great time, thanks for everything," rang out. It had been a weekend very much to everyone's liking.

Those two Freddys still worry me, though.

Mike and Jim

Seymour in Winter

So what would you do? It was 4:10 p.m. The light was fading fast. My altimeter indicated 3,600 feet. The summit was at 4,125. I was bone tired. My legs ached with each step. The forecast was for freezing rain.

We were on a snow-covered slide that got steeper and steeper. Every few yards there was another icy outcrop that had to be hunched over. Thank God for the saber-toothed crampons on my Sherpa snowshoes.

Mike and Jim were ahead, urging that it would get easier soon. I believed them, but I wasn't having fun anymore. So I said, "I'll see you guys back at Ward Brook lean-to. Have a nice climb," or something to that effect. I turned around and took my first notice of the view. There was a forested valley brown with leafless trees, green with firs, all embedded in a white background of snow. In the distance were other peaks.

Going down was definitely easier, but hurt my knees more. The snowshoes slid like skis if I leaned back; weight forward they bit into ice and rock. At least that's what they did when things went right. Several times I sat down or fell to one side to slow my descent.

I thought I was almost back to the lean-to when I could no longer see snowshoe prints. I thought I could make out the camp through the dim remaining light. I was ready to "just go for it," but I remembered Jim's admonition, "Stay on the trail." So I turned on my "trusty" Chouinard headlamp and saw that those shadows were not our lean-to. The trail, however, could be seen and following it another few hundred yards brought me safely there.

Mike and Jim had only a few peaks to go to complete their forty-six over 4,000 feet, in winter. They had long since done them in summer. Mike was moving to California soon and he was determined to finish this winter.

They belong to a group of elite winter mountain climbers in our Niagara Frontier chapter, which I had long considered accompanying. I held off because they are a hardy, gung ho bunch, younger than me and I was afraid that I could not keep up. I was right to hesitate. Those guys are tough.

We had driven into the parking lot at the Ward Brook trailhead late Friday night. We had come east on Route 3 through Tupper Lake and turned south through Cowries on the Stony Creek Ponds Road. The road had been traveled but it was slippery. Twice in the three miles from the bridge to the lot we had to get out and push. We debated whether we should stay there or go back to the parking area at the bridge. The forecast was for warmer weather and we feared getting the car stuck in the melting snow.

We opted for the bridge where we slept alongside the cars, in our bivey sacks, with the promise of pancakes in Tupper Lake in the morning. They tucked me in with a mildly disquieting story of trying to sleep in a similar arrangement on another trip. They had just gotten off to sleep when Bob Grim and a bunch of hard-driving climbers from the Albany chapter came roaring into the parking lot. They weren't run over, but the engines were left running and our guys had to get up or be asphyxiated.

That was OK because Grim and company made up for it with tips like the one that led to this trip. Bob had called Jim and told him he had been up Seymour the previous weekend. The snow wasn't too deep and they had left us a trail right to the sign-in cylinder on the top.

After breakfast we drove back to the trailhead with the plan of leaving our packs there and returning the car to the bridge 3.3 miles back. I jumped at the chance to guard the packs rather than walk the extra three miles.

When I was considering this trip, I called Mike and Jim and talked it over at some length. We have been on other trips together canoeing and hiking in warmer weather. They seemed to think that I would be able to handle it. They seemed pleased to have me and they offered to make it easier, if necessary, by giving me minimal trail breaking duties.

I made only the third member of their party. For safety the usual minimum is four. Mike said that, "Two would be cutting it kind of thin."

We had had some previous discussions about pack weight. I had been to three sessions of ADK's Winter School and there I carried about seventy-five pounds. They felt that was outrageous. I had mixed feelings about it myself. Covering any distance with that weight is grueling, but having those reserves of equipment is very reassuring.

Jim explained that they went as light as possible, but they carried the same packs all the way to the summit rather than shifting to daypacks for their final ascent. That way they could go to their limit, stop anywhere and be relatively comfortable.

Jim advised me to get a good bivey sack because they do not bring a tent. Mike corrected that saying that he brings a lightweight tent without a bottom, but they rarely use it.

It was the arrival of my new two-hundred-dollar, solid Gore-Tex, REI, bivey sack on Thursday afternoon that prompted me to call Mike and make a commitment for the trip the next day. I wasn't going to spend that kind of money for equipment and just look at it.

While moving, on the trail, these two wear polypro long underwear with an outer shell of Gore-Tex jackets and pants. They do without an insulating layer until they stop. For insulation I brought an extra set of long underwear, a pair of pile pants, and a big down parka. On other trips I had brought more insulating clothing of pile or wool enough for a complete change. They feel that their sleeping bags provide their reserve of insulation if they get wet.

Both brought vapor-barrier liners for their sleeping bags, which they say, add another ten or twenty degrees of warmth.

We all had Koflach plastic double boots and wore them with two pair of socks, one of wool and one of polypro. We used vapor barrier socks for greater warmth and in an attempt to keep the loden insulation of the inner boot dry.

We had tubular, aluminum Sherpa snowshoes, mine with the big fang crampons, theirs with the lower profile aluminum triangles. Jim and I brought ski poles. Mike doesn't think the extra arm leverage is worth the added weight.

We had Insulite sleeping pads and plastic ground cloths, two MSR stoves each with a pint of fuel, extra socks, extra mittens, goggles, whistles, maps, cigarette lighters, etc. Each carried his own food, mostly carbohydrate, minimal cooking kits, and a quart and a half of water.

We decided we would not need crampons. I went through my usual stuff and cut it to the minimum. I did not bring rescue flares, a second flashlight, much spare food, reading or writing materials, or a candle. I even stripped down my first-aid kit. My pack weighed thirty-five manageable pounds. The chief weight saving was probably fewer clothes, less food, and the lack of a tent.

As I waited in the parking lot, to keep from being too guilty and cold, I ferried the packs along the trail a ways. The packs were all Lowe internal frames. Jim's was the heaviest, I think closer to forty-five than thirty-five pounds.

The walk through the woods was pretty. There was snow on the overhanging scrub spruce and a few inches of powder on top of several already packed on the trail. Glacial erratics were scattered about. There were birch and beech and some very mature spruce and hemlock. Alongside of one crick a huge boulder had a big, old, dead beech sitting on top of it with six-inch roots imprisoning the rock. An old hemlock was blown over, upending the root system, so that it formed a twirling, mossy green and root wall beside the trail.

There are several log bridges to cross. That is a little tricky on snowshoes. Sometimes I sidestepped, other times I was able to stride the two logs with snowshoes side by side. It helped when there was a stack of snow on top of the logs.

The first two hours I hung back and the other guys broke trail. It bothered me a little that I was letting them do all the work, but neither of them said anything. They did get a ways ahead of me at times, but they'd wait up after a bit.

We'd chat, have some water, eat a couple of gumdrops, and move on. Finally I took the lead. There wasn't that much snow, but for what it was worth, I broke trail for an hour.

We had about a five-and-a-half-mile hike to Ward Brook lean-to from the trailhead. There was a gradual rise of about six hundred feet, but mostly it was flat. We crossed the horse trail, passed Blueberry Pond and its lean-to and arrived at Ward Brook lean-to at 2:30 p.m., five hours after Mike and Jim had left the car.

We stopped and admired the Ward Brook lean-to. It has a new wood floor, shelves on either wall, many convenient hanging nails, a clothesline strung through eyehooks along the main rafter, and a logbook. The three of us want to compliment "Jungle" Jim Mosher and Fred Cady, along with Jim's wife Becky and their daughter, Ashley, who are taking care of the place under ADK's "Adopt a Lean-to" program. As Jim put it, "The place shows a real proprietary interest."

It was here that I was confused for a minute. Jim pulled out his bivey sack, sleeping bag and pad, and said, "I've got to rest a bit before we go up." We still had about a mile and a half and 2,000 feet to go to get to the top of trail-less Seymour. I was fairly tired, but for a moment I thought Jim was tireder. Then I figured it out. It was a joke. Jim was just dumping out his gear to make a daypack out of the compression sack for his sleeping bag and he was raring to go.

This did represent a change in the plan, as I understood it. I didn't argue about not taking full packs to the summit, but I was unsure about wanting to go up there with minimal equipment that late. My weary muscles won the argument and I kept my mouth shut.

I emptied my pack and squeezed it tight with its compression straps. I thought I could put my lower half in the pack if we spent the night out. I packed my parka, a ground cloth, some food, water, a few emergency items, and away we went.

The usual approach follows a creek that crosses the trail one-tenth of a mile beyond our lean-to. We found Bob Grim's snowshoe tracks turning off there and we followed them up.

After parting company I got back to the lean-to about five and my headlamp flickered out. The bulb was fitting loosely. When I attempted to repair it in the dark it came apart and was a total loss. Oh, how I wished I had brought along my usual, small, Lithium-powered, backup light.

My MSR stove, with its built-in sparkler-starter, lit like a charm. I left the aluminum windshield off to give me light. My water supply was used up. I proceeded to melt snow for fresh water.

By the flickering light I changed into a dry undershirt, pulled on my pile pants, crawled into my down parka, and waited for the return of the rest of the crew. Their headlamps came bobbing along out of the black about 6:30.

They were pleased at my water supplies. Mike loaned me a flashlight. I hadn't felt like eating. With company, rest, and light I found an appetite.

I had a bagel with jam, hot raspberry Jell-O, spicy beef stick, and a big plastic bag full of hot reconstituted noodles, potatoes, and beans. Jim had freeze-dried lasagna and all through the night he kept eating ham sandwiches and little cherry pies. Mike had been experimenting with a dehydrator he got for Christmas. He had a pot of water to which he added dried mushrooms, peppers, carrots, lentils and such, then noodles, soup, and a big chunk of roast beef. He ate rather silently commenting only once that, "It lacks something."

The beef was leftover from our dinner at the Barnes Corners Hotel on Tug Hill. Mike and Jim had never been there. They were a little put off by the tumbled-down, tarpaper shack exterior of the place. They were ready to get back in the car at the "Leave all fire arms outside" sign. But inside we were given such huge portions of meat, vegetables, fresh rolls, potatoes, and gravy that I suspect it will be placed on the regular itinerary. Jim thinks that the Barnes Corners plan of putting three kinds of pie on the salad bar ought to be made the legal standard in New York State. Mike was the only one of us who ate his entire plateful of food. It was my leftover beef that he lugged along in a doggy bag to grace his stew in camp.

We were in our sacks by 8 p.m. I slept well, waking a few times to listen to the howling wind that was bringing in a new weather front. I woke finally at 5 and got up at 5:30. I made breakfast, ate breakfast, melted more snow, rattled pots and pans, packed all my gear and never got a rise out of the other two. So I broke out the Ward Brook lean-to logbook and read for a while and then wrote one of the longest entries in it. By then it started raining pretty good, as well as blowing. All the snow was turning to slush. At long last about 8 Mike and Jim came to.

I took a head start leaving at 9 a.m. As soon as I got on the trail the sore muscles were apparent. I had heard of *mal de raquette*, a French Canadian expression for the soreness of your upper calf that snow shoeing produces. This was it.

About 10 the guys caught up with me. We hiked together most of the way but I took up my tail gunner position and eventually lost them in the distance. I passed the time enjoying the scenery and freedom from routine. When I got tired I took my mind off it by rehearsing my lines and cues for a play I am supposed to be in next month. By 2:30 we were back at the car, damp, clothes steaming and muscles tender.

The trip was fun. It was a lot of work. It made me clearer on my limitations. Mike and Jim are stronger than I. Their extra physical stamina gives them an edge that lets them cut safety precautions a little thinner.

I was pleasantly surprised when they invited me to come with them the next weekend. Mike said, wryly, "We've got a really great plan to do four peaks and the best thing about it is that no one leg of the trip is very strenuous." I thanked them saying I was going to rest up. I didn't tell them that I probably wouldn't even be standing up straight by then.

I can enjoy a trip with them when we go with the understanding that my capacity is not the same as theirs. The weekends on which they are stretching their limits I intend to stay home or travel with the non-elite crowd that are more my speed.

I guess I envy them. I don't think I was ever quite in their class physically but when I was running five miles a day I know I was quicker than now. Back then I had a lot less time to spend in the woods. So there is some compensation.

I never was the toughest kid on the block or the smartest in class or the fastest, but I could give some of them a run for their money and I enjoyed being in the action. "It is not whether you win or lose, it's how you play the game," isn't it?

Damn it, I wish I could out walk those two punks.

Root-bound erratic long the Ward Brook Trail.

All set to go except for the stomach.

Fuel Bottle Blues
or
Single vs. Double Portage

"Where were you last night?" you ask.

"I was out in the woods burping Coleman Fuel — God damn it!"

Dick and I had been planning this weeklong canoe trip for six months. He and I have done a lot of traveling together but there are some depths to his personality I never really understood till we wound up together in this pinch.

We get along pretty well canoe tripping. The only difference we have is on whether we will make single or double portages. I like to travel light and make one carry between lakes. He likes to bring a full-sized axe and maybe even his kitchen sink in his pack but he doesn't mind making two trips when we portage.

He picked me up at 5:30 in the morning. I thought I was all packed and ready to go. We tied my canoe on the roof of his van. But when I went to throw my canoe-pack inside the van, I smelled Coleman Fuel. The stove inside of my pack had leaked and my gear was soaked with it.

I quickly repacked, salvaging what I could of my gear. The food looked OK. It was all double bagged, in plastic. I had to grab a different sleeping bag but I thought I was set.

We spent the first night at a campground, in tents, alongside the van. We ate a late supper. Dick ate mostly ice cream from the store. I made a cheese sandwich with supplies from home. The cheese tasted a little funny.

In the morning we each made our own breakfast. I had coffee, oatmeal and raisins, from the supplies in my pack. Then I began burping. Each burp left in my mouth the unmistakable aftertaste and after smell of Coleman Fuel.

I sniffed the rest of my food and could not be sure. But Dick, whose nose was less contaminated, said that all my food smelled of Coleman Fuel. The plastic bags apparently were no barrier to it.

I thought a little, then threw it all into the bear-proof garbage shed. I continued to burp, my stomach started to burn, I felt nauseous and I began to worry. I wondered if psychology was working this on me or if these were real pharmacological effects of the fuel. Then my imagination took off, what is going to happen to my liver, how about my brain?

Dick was sympathetic and reassuring, though he couldn't resist a little laugh and a remark about not breathing too near the flame of our camp stove.

We went to the outfitter's store in camp to ask advice and possibly buy more food. The proprietor took on an authoritative air and seemed to try to be genuinely helpful. "People commonly inhale Coleman Fuel and gasoline to get intoxicated. If you get enough of it in your system it can cause brain damage but just swallowing a little bit, it shouldn't cause you no harm," he said.

Then he added, teasing a little, "If you had enough in you, you'd be confused and your pupils would be dilated." He squinted closely at my pupils, "You aren't confused are you...What's two and two?"

Dick said, "No, no he's always like this."

The proprietor went on, "Oh yes, I can remember a lot of trips, the butter and sometimes the bread would get that flavor into them and you'd burp a little gas but it was no problem."

"What'd I tell you," said Dick.

"So, I'm not going to die?" I said.

The proprietor slapped me on the back with a laugh, "No, friend, you're not going to die— Maybe a little upset stomach. I remember one time a good customer of mine got bit by a snake. He come running in here and took two big shots of what he thought was vodka. Of course by the time the first one was down he realized it wasn't. Right away he vomited it back up. He got a lot more in him then you did, and all he got out of it was an upset stomach."

I was starting to regain confidence, and then he told this story. "This fella I knew once, he was filling up his gas tank from a pump. The gas refluxed back all over his arm, do you see. So his arm was soaked. He wiped it off on a rag, the best way he could. He went driving off. Then he lit up a cigarette...His whole arm went up in flames. He was waving it out the window, trying to put it out...Wouldn't you know, a DEC Ranger from Tupper Lake cited him for 'BRANDISHING A FIRE ARM,'— ha, ha, ha!"

He and Dick whooped it up on that one. Then he good-naturedly sold me twenty dollars worth of food for forty-seven dollars. I was not totally reassured.

We got our canoes across one lake and one portage before I gave in to my worries and my sick stomach and told Dick, "I gotta' go home."

Good old Dick, he couldn't have been more understanding. He drove us the 300 miles home without complaint.

I called him the next day. I told him, "I talked to my doctor. He said not to worry. He didn't even want to do any tests."

"I'm glad to hear that," Dick said.

"I double checked. I looked it up in my *Merck Manual.* Ingesting a small quantity won't hurt you. Inhaling is dangerous."

"Well, that's good," he said.

"Dick, thanks for putting up with me. OK?"

"You don't have to thank me," he said. "I was relieved when you said you wanted to go home. I was trying to figure out how I would get your body out of there if you died. I didn't think I could single portage you, the way you like. I thought I might have to bring you out in two trips."

*Logging cabin at Aldrich Settlement where
the Beahans lived after they left the Little River.*

Little River Christmas

"Cra-crack, crack, crack, cra-crack," the axes rang as the regular pattern of several axemen's strokes intermingled irregularly. Then a moment of silence after Mike MacChecny roared out in his mocking bass "Tiii—mmmber." There was another longer cracking sound that echoed off the cliff on the other side of the Little River and a crackling whoosh as the ancient tree leaned and, gathering speed, fell through the branches of its neighbors. A final satisfying thump and bounce marked the end of its long natural life and the beginning of its commercial use.

Mike glowed with pride as he wiped the sweat from his forehead. He had pulled off his mackinaw and his woolen shirt. He stood there in heavy woolen pants, high caulked boots and disreputable damp long johns. The tree had landed right where he wanted, largely by skill, but luck always played a hand in the woods.

Ivan Harney and Bert Patchin, a few yards away, finished sawing a tree into the standard thirteen-foot, four-inch logs the buyers required. They tramped through two inches of snow toward Mike. Bert, the younger of the two, carried a double-bitted axe by its head. Ivan, with their two-man, crosscut saw over his shoulder hollered, "Goll-ly what a relief, I thought you was goin' to drop that one on us for sure. What'a ya tryin' ta do, chop the whole woods down today?"

Bert had on an old felt hat of his father's and a turtleneck sweater. Ivan wore a brimmed cap and wool shirt. They carried their jackets, which were not nearly as elegant as Mike's sheepskin-lined mackinaw.

Mike laughed. "No, I'm just feelin' my oats and tryin' ta get rich. Christmas is next week. 'Tis the season to be jolly."

Ivan shouted back, "I'm goin' to do my jolly down at Casey's Saturday night."

"You better watch how much of that kickapoo joy juice you wrap yourself around or your old lady is goin' to park your moccasins out in the snow. John Whalen didn't take it too lightly neither, your callin' him a horse's fanny last Saturday."

The Casey family ran a boarding house and saloon at Aldrich where the men from the Aldrich Mill could sleep, drink, and get a beefsteak. It was only a mile and a half walk down the railroad from the Beahan Little River camp. The saloon was a sore temptation. The challenge lay in staying out of a fight down there and staying out of the river on the walk back in the dark with a belly full of whiskey.

"Aw, come on Mike, you've been a wet blanket since you took the Pledge. A fella has to cut loose once't in a while. Move over, the kid and me got work to do."

Mike stepped back to rest a second. Bert hopped on the downed tree to skin off the lower branches. He was proud of the new high leather boots his pa bought him. Newt Jonas made them to order in his shop at Great Bend. The sharp caulks covering their soles gave him a grip as he walked the trunk. He remembered his pa saying, "Now you can ride them logs with the best of us river pigs. You won't need to take no swimmin' lessons, neither."

"Swack, swack" one branch fell to the strokes of his axe. Then "swack, bang" and a loud ring. "Kee—riste, watch whatch'er doin'," yelled Ivan as the axe flew through the air within two feet of his head.

"Eeeyoow—Jesus, Mother of Joseph," yelled Bert, "I'm cut."

He was hopping on one foot with both hands holding his left lower leg. Mike and Ivan got him down off the tree. They sat him on Mike's coat and took a look at the leg. The razor-sharp axe had neatly incised his woolen pant leg and put a bloody gash in his calf.

Ivan pulled out his blue bandanna and laid it on the leg.

Mike extracted a wad from his cheek and deposited it on a maple leaf. He started working on a fresh plug. "What we need is some witchhopple to stick the backie on with."

"We ain't goin' to find no special medicine leaf this time of year. We'll just have to make do with what we got. Gee kid, you could'a killed me. Your pa taught you better'n that!"

"I'm awful sorry Ivan, I never done that before."

"Well you better be," said Ivan.

"Do you think I'll be laid up with this? I was s'posed to mind the teams while the Beahans went down home for Christmas."

Mike mushed the two wads of tobacco onto a couple of large maple leaves and applied the mess to Bert's leg. "You best think about restin' up for a couple of weeks and try not to let this thing fester on you."

Ivan tied his bloody bandanna tightly around Bert's leg. "That oughta keep the bleedin' down till you can get ta Carthage ta see Dr. Lawler. He might be able ta stitch it fer ya."

Mike stood up and yelled to Joe Moses who was working his team just up the muddy path. He had been trying to get in some early log skidding but there wasn't enough snow to do much. "Frenchie, come on over here with your outfit, the kid just took a hunk of meat out'a his leg. Maybe you can get him back to camp before he bleeds to death."

Bert shuddered, covering his fear with a game smile. "Thanks, Mr. MacChecny, and thank you, Ivan. I guess I really messed up."

Frenchie had moved quickly and he overheard this. "Don' worry 'bout it, keed, I seen dees palookas screw up tres grand plen-ty.

"Ivan, you help heem up on Ned," indicating the bigger of his dapple-gray pair. "He ride you easy. He be *un bon cheval.*"

John Beahan, a rangy 6-foot 2-inch Irishman with brown hair and a big handlebar mustache, was just coming out of the barn when he saw Frenchie and his team bringing Bert up the road. "Goll—ly," he mumbled the severest curse he allowed himself, "what in the devil?"

The Beahan compound was stretched along one side of the road that ambled down from Aldrich, crossed the Little River on a corduroy bridge and then went on toward Star Lake. All the buildings were of logs chinked with moss and mud. The big double barn with a roof between the two halves to shelter hay had stalls for sixteen horses. Then came the big sleeping camp. Next was the main camp. One end of it was partitioned off with curtains for sleeping quarters for John and his family. The rest of it was devoted to a long dining table for the men and a kitchen with a big wood cook stove. A little back of the main camp was Tom and Minnie's place.

John was the oldest of the Beahan brothers up there. Bill, his senior, argued with their old man and went west ten years earlier. He last wrote from Chicago. Bart and Tom were partners with John in jobbing lumber. Bart was a bachelor. John and Liva lived in the main camp with their youngest daughter Bessie. Their older kids, Susie and Leo, stayed in Carthage winters, with Aunt Mary and Uncle Newt Jonas. They went to school there and then, summer vacations, came up to the camp along with their cousins Rose and Alton.

Tom, his wife Minnie, and their three kids, Raymond, Geneva and Laurence, had a small log camp to themselves up back of the main camp.

Twenty-five or thirty lumberjacks and teamsters lived in the big sleeping camp. Liva, Minnie and a hired girl fed them at the long table in the main camp.

They were in touch with the outside world by way of the Carthage and Adirondack branch of the New York Central Railroad. There was a

station at Aldrich a mile and a half away. The kids looked forward to the
weekly funny papers coming in on the train on Mondays. Staples were
brought in that way and there was the occasional luxury of a trip home.

"Minnie, Liva," John called towards the main camp. "Bert Patchin's
hurt. He needs some nursin'." The two women hurried out looking worried

Minnie Beahan and Gramma Gifford

as Joe came up to them with Bert still up on Ned. John helped him to get
down and hobble inside.

"I'm awful sorry to be all this bother," Bert said. He looked pale and
ashamed. "My Ma'll skin me alive."

"Don't you worry, I know your ma, she'll be worried sick and spoil
you rotten over this," said Liva. She helped him onto the dining table.

Little Bessie stuck her head out between the curtains dividing off the sleeping area. Ivan stepped over to her, chucking her under the chin."

"How's my girl? What you been doin'?"

"Oh, just my lessons," she glowed. "What's wrong with Bert?"

"He'll be all right, just mistook his leg for a tree and took a hunk off it. Looks like he'll get an early Christmas."

"Are you OK, Bert? Does it hurt?"

"Well, it don't tickle but I'm still breathing," said Bert, making a face at the little girl.

Minnie came over with a basin of hot water and a gray linen hand towel. She washed away the blood and spare tobacco juice, then gently undid the bandanna and peered at the oozing wound.

"Nothing for that but to keep the poultice on and keep it bound up tight," said Liva. "You ain't goin' to be fit for much but layin' in bed and eatin' Christmas puddin' for awhile." Then she turned to John and said, "I think we better see about getting this boy ta home as soon as we can."

"But who will take care of the teams while you folks are doin' your Christmas visitin'?" cried Bert. "I can't go home now."

John said, "We'll tend to the horses. You have to take care of that leg."

Next morning, Joe Moses took Bert to the Aldrich terminal and put him on board the 8:25 for Carthage. John had him wire ahead to have Bert's family meet him at the station. There was no Workers Compensation, just "the breaks of the game."

That December night in 1905, the Beahans had a family conference. They had planned, for weeks, a Christmas break to visit their folks, the Giffords and Jonases in Carthage, along the Black River and up on Tug Hill. They had lived in the Yousey camp since 1900 and had little opportunity for socializing. There was timber to cut and skid, men to feed, and babies to be born and tended. They were lonesome and homesick, especially Minnie.

Minnie Gifford was Tom's second wife. He was ten years older. She had been the apple of her father, Nick Gifford's, eye. As a girl in Pinckney up on Tug Hill she had her own one-horse shay with a buffalo robe and a pretty little filly named Nell to pull it.

She was very taken by Tom Beahan's good manners, loving attention and impressed by his considerable reading, despite his rough lumberman exterior. But after three kids in five years in a log shack in the woods she was wearing down. She had her heart set on an old fashioned Christmas on the Gifford farm at Pinckney. The news that Bert wouldn't be around to tend the teams over Christmas was heartbreaking.

John spoke first. He had methodically lit his clay pipe and taken several puffs. The pipe stem was broken off short, John's precaution against its breaking off too short. "It's tough luck for Bert getting hurt. We will have to pray he comes through it OK. Tough for us, too. I don't think we can expect Frenchie Joe to stay up here alone to tend the horses. I've already promised the men a Christmas ta home. They been up here pretty steady since September."

Barty said, "I don't know but what I could manage it John, it ain't that bad."

"Minnie's the one who deserves a break," said Liva. "Why don't we stay and she and Tom and the kids go on home."

Tom put in, "We agreed to share and share alike. You've been up here as long as we have. It wouldn't be fair."

Minnie's face fell. You could see she had been crying. She said nothing, just went on mending a thick woolen sock.

John spoke up again "It would save us quite a piece of change if we passed up this trip. The C and A Railroad ain't for free and we could use the time to mend up harness and get our tools in shape for the big winter push. This contract we got off the Youseys and McDonalds ain't near as sweet as it looked on paper. If we get out of here with much more than our shirts next year we'll have to call ourselves lucky."

Tom put an arm around Minnie, "Next Christmas we'll be home, Mama. You can count on it."

She buried her head in his shoulder, "I sure hope so, Tommie."

Wouldn't you know it? Just at that moment old Engine 97 passing through Aldrich Station let out a long lonesome wail, enough to rend the heart of the hardest businessman in the lumber trade.

John knocked the ash out of his pipe, brushed it through a knothole in the pine board floor and said, "Well, that's it then, we stay put and have our Christmas in the woods. We still got a couple of fat hens that should make good eatin'. I think the treasury can spring for some candied fruit and nuts for one of Minnie's famous rum cakes."

"No reason we can't have some celebrating around here."

"Barty, you think there are any turkeys left over to Streeter Lake where we saw them last summer?"

The next several days, felling and skidding slowed to a halt as the

Minnie Beahan "horsing around," glad to finally be out of the woods.

men took off in twos and threes for a few days of rest and catching up on family life.

John, Bart and Tom tended to the harnesses, horses, and tools. The ladies got a little breathing spell with most of the men out of camp and not needing to be fed four times a day. Minnie got a letter off to her folks with the bad news. Liva wrote to Aunt Mary giving her instructions to buy a new shirt and a jackknife for Leo and a doll and a dress for Susie and to give them a special hug and kiss from her for Christmas.

The kids remembered it as a good time because the grown ups weren't quite so busy. Tom took six-year-old Raymond out to track deer and he let him practice a few shots with his 38 Winchester.

Bessie, who was eight, got permission to take her younger cousins, Geneva and Laurence, down to the giant oat bin in the barn where she loved to jump in and bury herself. One night John and Raymond went out to the root house to catch the raccoon that had been raiding their stores. Ray held the lantern. His uncle, John, put on some long heavy canvas gloves. Inside in the semi-dark up in the rafters a pair of brazen eyes shined at them. John wrestled with the coon and the next night the coon was feeding the family instead of vice versa.

On the Saturday night before Christmas, Liva let Bessie help bake pies for breakfast. She made a special one for Ivan Harney who loved pie almost as much as Bessie loved him. He had a little girl back home and Bessie put him in mind of her. Anyway he made over her every chance he could and she delighted in the attention. She was John and Liva's youngest and her specialty was being cute.

Sunday at breakfast Ivan didn't show up. Bessie was all set to serve him his special apple pie with "Ivan" carved across the top and dosed with extra cinnamon the way he liked it.

Ivan had been spending part of his rest time at Casey's before going home. That night he came back to camp very late. Bessie was told he was sick. At noon she was allowed to make a trip into the sleeping camp with a mug of coffee and the pie for him.

She found him in sorry shape. He was still half-asleep. His nose was swollen and his chest was torn where a caulked boot had kicked him. He broke into a pained smile when Bessie came in with her treat and said, "What'cha lookin' at, Honey? You should see how the other guy looks." That was the only breakfast in bed in the recorded history of the camp.

"Can we have a Christmas tree this year?" the children chorused at supper two nights before the great day.

"Oh, that's a lot of bother," John grumbled.

"But it adds so much ta the spirit," Minnie objected. "We always had one ta home. It smells so good ta have a fresh tree in the house."

Raymond chimed in, "All the kids in the comics have Christmas trees. Please, please can't we have one?"

Tom said, "John, I think we better have a tree."

John shook his head and put up his hands in surrender.

Tom turned to the rest in a businesslike way, "If Bessie and Ray help me pick one out, I'll cut it down and drag it back but Barty has got to stand it up in here for us somehow."

The children danced around yelling "Hooray, hooray." Bart stuck out his hand to Tom and said, "You got a done deal."

Later Tom and the kids brought home a nice full scrub spruce from the middle of a meadow. Barty took over. He trimmed off a few lower branches and tried setting the tree up in a bucket. That didn't work. He started to tie it from a line over one of the rafters but everyone objected, "You can't 'hang' a Christmas tree."

Finally it dawned on him. John's ashtray, that knothole in the floor at the end of the table, would do it. He pared the main stem with his draw-shave, stuck it through the hole and announced, "Thar she be, slicker'n a whistle."

"Bart, you're a genius," said Liva. "You should'a been a engineer. Ain't she pretty."

That night they strung cranberries and popcorn on strands to decorate the tree. Just before bedtime Liva got out her Christmas candles and clipped twelve of them on the tree. Minnie was persuaded to play a jig on her mouth organ and then "Silent Night." Then, with the children pleading, the grownups finally consented to a few minutes of lighting the tree. It sparkled in beauty and warmth as the family gathered round, held hands and John led a prayer.

Liva had gotten a bucket of water standing close by. "This 'minds me of the time the roof started on fire around my stove chimney and I ran out screaming for help. You remember, John? You were working an axe handle or something and you had to light up that darn pipe of yours while you were calculating how to put out my fire."

They all had a good laugh, put out the candles and went to bed. The next day was Christmas Eve. At noon there was the unexpected sound of sleigh bells as a livery team from Casey's came pulling up. Lo and behold, if it wasn't Gramma and Grampa Gifford and Aunt Edie with a load of treats and presents from civilization.

Minnie, with the kids close in her skirts, ran out to them weeping for joy.

Grampa Gifford jumped down and grabbed her in a big bear hug. "How's my sweet little girl? I couldn't keep your mother away when we got your letter."

"Oh, Papa, it is so good to see you. We are goin' ta have the best Christmas we ever had."

Barty took the horses in the barn for a rubdown while the others went inside. And they did have a most memorable Christmas.

It wasn't till late that summer when the men were peeling pulp that Nick Gifford had the courage to write Minnie and tell her he had had to sell old Nell to pay for that Christmas visit.

Little River Portage

"Why sure. You can make it through from Star Lake to Aldrich, now. May be a few blowdowns."

"Great!"

"Old Mr. Schuler died. He left his place to Clarkson University. They sold it to the State."

"Oh yeah?"

"Lot of people want to try it. You'll be the first ones."

By golly, that was just what I was looking for, the chance to be first on something. But I hadn't paid enough attention to the blowdown part. It would have been smart to ask Bernie Suskevitch a few more questions.

I called my son, Nick, in Vermont. "Let's sneak in a canoe trip, before the black flies wake up."

"Great. Where to?"

"I just got off the phone with Bernie Suskevitch, the ranger at Wanakena. That Schuler inholding, the one that blocked the Little River portage, it belongs to the state now. We can paddle past Grampa's old camp."

"Let's do it."

We met at the Cranberry Lake Inn on a Friday night early in May. The weather was damp and blustery. The Inn had a "For Sale" sign. An elderly couple were stretching out a meal in the dining room and two fishermen were watching TV with the barmaid. A waitress greeted us with, "Sorry, no prime rib tonight."

We enjoyed our spaghetti and meatballs and caught each other up on family doings. These outings with my kids are better than visiting at home. They let us live together 24 hours a day; eat, sleep, paddle, hike, argue and talk. If you do that with a stranger for a few days, they get to be like family. With family they become people again, not just voices at the other end of "your preferred-long-distance-carrier."

After dinner, the manager fiddled with the electric heater in our room so that it finally warmed up enough to take off our pile and fleece. We poured over topo maps for the Oswegatchie and Little Rivers. Nick agreed to my plan, a first-time trip from Star Lake to Aldrich portaging the falls of the Little River. In route we would pass the site of the old Yousey logging camp where Nick's granddad was born. That accomplished, we would paddle the east branch of the Oswegatchie on Sunday, Monday and Tuesday. We thought we might make it a distance above High Falls in that much time.

Next morning, we were ordering pancakes at the Stone Manor Diner across from the Inn. I said, "We ought to stop at Wanakena and let Suskevitch know we are actually going to do this trip."

"Sure," Nick answered. He wasn't paying much attention. He was busy negotiating for fruit in our pancakes. The cook was all out of blueberries but she offered to try adding strawberry-sundae topping to the batter. These pancakes gave us plenty of carbohydrates but if you are ever in that situation consider having the strawberries on top instead of inside.

At Wanakena, Bernie was cordial and enthusiastic. He came out of his front-porch office into the light rain with a cud of tobacco in his cheek. He inspected our canoe and us in our big rubber boots, Gore-Tex hats, and rain suits and our canoe. He spat and wished us well.

"We're going in off Young's Road back of Star Lake," I said.

"You'll be the first ones."

Nick asked, "Any special way to do the portage?"

"Keep an eye out for what's left of the footbridge. Then get out at the concrete abutments of the old Schuler Road Bridge beyond that. You best get out there on the north side. Some folks got lost on them roads down on the south side last year."

"With a canoe?" I asked.

"No. Walking. You ought to walk up the road to take a look at the Schuler cabin."

That seemed to pin things down. We presumed we could carry up the road to the cabin, keep on going and put in below the falls, a big presumption. We had read Paul Jamison's excellent description of the Little River. He paddled up the river from Aldrich to the western edge of the inholding and he also paddled down to its other edge from Star Lake. But he had never traversed the forbidden segment itself so he did not describe what lay between.

We had not bothered to ask Bernie whether he had inspected that in-between part, either. He must have felt that he had covered that point, by conceding to us the honor of being first. Playing the bold voyageurs as we did, he probably thought that we thought we knew what we were getting into.

I had tucked in the back of my mind an image of the Schuler inholding road. As I remembered, it looped briefly from the river at the inholding bridge, back to the river beyond the falls, while its main route ran past Readaway Ponds up to Star Lake. It seemed a royal road past the falls and a bailout option if it did not work as a portage.

We drove the Coffins Mills road out of Oswegatchie Village to Aldrich. We planned to drop one of our two cars along the woods road that follows the bed of the old Carthage and Adirondack Railroad. The road parallels a stretch of the Little River, near Aldrich, before bearing off to Streeter Lake. The road was, ominously, gated. There were signs giving mileage, prohibiting camping and warning of wind damage.

As we drove back toward Star Lake, I said, "Nice name, Coffins Mills. Sounds grim."

"No. It's just a common New England name," Nick said. I was reassured. At least he wasn't spooked.

We loaded our seventeen-foot Kevlar Wenona with enough gear to get us through the night, in a pinch. We put it into the water where the Little River passes under Young's Road. Within fifty yards we were lifting over

Nick below the falls of the Little River.

and working around blowdowns. Within one hundred and fifty we were in what seemed to us an impenetrable jungle growing out of the water.

"See that yellow blaze?" Nick said. "Maybe that's a portage around this stuff."

"Maybe, let's take a look."

We looked and we looked and we climbed blowdown and crawled over slash left from salvage logging and we found no clear way by land or water. Here and there we found patches of yellow paint and some sections of skid road. We got separated. Near somebody's old camp, Nick finally found water that bore some resemblance to river but seemed to have no way to get to it. We found each other, using our whistles, went back for the canoe and by turns threaded and wrestled it through blowdown, slash and brush into water. Later we realized that those yellow blazes had nothing to do with a portage. They were state property lines.

There followed a peaceful interlude of paddling with only a few ordinary blowdowns and strainers. We never did identify Tamarack Creek that should have joined the river at about our second put-in. We also did not see the remains of the old footbridge. We did start to hear some roaring water and we noted the walls of the riverbank rising into a canyon ahead. Then, we saw what remained of the Schuler Road Bridge. Marvelously alerted by that roar, we exited just above the bridge and began our carry. The 1500 pace canoe carry, on the road, was a pleasant contrast to the bushwhack.

As we walked along under the canoe something about the lay of the land made me wonder if I had read the map correctly. I said, "Do you suppose this road runs right down to the river on the other side of the falls?"

"I thought you said you saw that on a map somewhere."

"In Jamison's book...there looks like a kind of a loop of road from the bridge, back to the river," I answered.

"I hope you saw right."

A more careful look, later, showed that the loop was above the falls, not around them.

At the height-of-land we came out from under our canoe and set our packs down. We understood, right away, why old man Schuler was reluctant to share this place. It's an eagle's nest perched high above the roaring water of the falls. The cabin is without a roof but a few paces off the veranda and you are on a rocky outcrop. There, below, white foaming water pours out of a jagged rock crevasse. Downstream, boulders keep the water churning for a quarter of a mile. Green forest surrounds it all.

The sun had broken through and dried the grass tolerably. We took out bagels and cheddar cheese and we lay down to refresh ourselves. The view and our anticipated victory added relish to the meal.

A road does seem to continue on past the cabin down river. We hoisted our burdens and started on, negotiating one or two more blowdowns before finding the road to dead end in the woods. So we carried back to the cabin and did some scouting without our packs and canoe. A path leads from the cabin to a spring halfway down the canyon wall. An aluminum dipper still hangs at the spring. We worked our way to the canyon floor and boulder-hopped out into the river to get a full view of the waterfall. The rushing waters and giant rocks are a soothing, hypnotic sight. They held us there in awe for twenty minutes as we pondered how to get past them and the rapids that stretched beyond.

The tangled shore looked almost as tough as the tumbling river. We retreated up the canyon still dimly hoping for some road access to the river. We did find a road that looked promising. We followed it as it branched off the Schuler Road a few hundred yards north of the cabin. But several blowdowns later we came to its end, in woods. By then it was 3:30, so we decided to carry out by the road to Star Lake. It was about a mile and would not have been a bad carry except for our disappointment and weariness.

We stopped off at Wanakena. Bernie broke away from the gathering at the Saturday barbecue in the little park in front of his house. A light misty rain had begun again so the group was mostly huddled in the shelter.

"Did you make it?" he called as he approached.

"Nope," Nick responded.

"What happened?"

"It's a jungle from Young's Road over towards Schuler's," I put in.

"That so? It was all cleared out last year."

I shook my head, "It's a terrible mess now."

"And there's no way to get past the rapids, once you are around the falls," Nick added.

"You don't say. Well that's valuable information. Thanks for letting me know."

"I wouldn't advise anyone else to go that way, till it's cleared out a little better," I said.

"I don't know if they are going to do anything about that. You might want to write to the Unit Manager at Potsdam and see what you can get them to do."

"Have you ever been through there?" Nick asked.

Bernie moved the tobacco to his other cheek. "No, never have. Been to both ends. Not this year, though."

"We're going to try the Oswegatchie tomorrow," I said.

"That should be a lot easier, till you get up above High Falls. Had

Blowdown on upper section of Little River.

some people come through from Lowe's Lake the other day. The portage was clear but the river was pretty bad up above the falls."

Two years before, Nick and I had looked at the far end of the Lowe's-Lake-Oswegatchie portage right after the disastrous microburst blowdown had devastated the area. We could have walked the route five feet off the ground hopping from downed tree to downed tree, but no one could have gotten a canoe through there then. At least what we had been through along the Little River was nothing like that.

"We'll let you know if we come out alive," Nick added.

Bernie shook hands with us both and ducked for cover back toward the shelter. "See you."

Sunday the weather started bright and windy on the Oswegatchie but it was all clear paddling back and forth on its meanders. We rested at High Rock to wonder at the uprooted trees and admire fiddleheads and little yellow flowers blooming, hawks sailing, herons cruising, and little formations of ducks. As we paddled, a couple of nice big deer watched us, unafraid as we watched them.

We camped at the lean-to just beyond Griffins Rapids where the trail comes in from Cage Lake. I had spent a night there ten years before with my older son, Teck, on a hike from Aldrich to Wanakena by way of Cage Lake. An old map had led us to think that a bridge crossed the river there. A couple of fishermen in a canoe graciously saved us from an October swim by providing ferry service.

On the present trip, Nick and I ran into rain Sunday night and most of Monday. He was snug and dry in his tent, reading. I was pacing back and forth in the lean-to, itching to do something. Things looked even darker to me than they really were since I had forgotten my regular glasses and had to wear prescription sunglasses the whole time.

Nick said, "You know I slept in late this morning so that we'd be in the same time frame, in terms of perceived light."

"Thanks, a lot, Nick."

To pass the time, he read to us from the lean-to's thick logbook. There were tales of floods, mosquitoes, campfires, and good times. One entry was particularly intriguing. It was about someone being chased into a tree by a bear. When the victim licked the bear in a fair fight we began to realize that the story was about as reliable as Nick's reason for sleeping in.

Late that morning, at my urging, we took off upstream in the rain. It was still raining by midafternoon and we were damp, so damp we could feel the mildew growing inside of our rain suits. We voted and I won. So we headed back for dry beds at the Cranberry Lake Inn.

By the time we came to the take-out at Inlet the weather had changed into a beautiful sunshiny day. Just then the black flies came to. They bloomed in the sun and swarms descended upon us. We threw our canoe on the car roof. Unable to lash it properly, for the bugs in our eyes, ears and mouths, we put one line over the canoe and dashed out of the swarming area.

The next day, Tuesday, we still had half a day, so we put on head nets and walked back to explore the Little River portage sans canoe. It is an easy walk from Star Lake, past the pretty Readaway Ponds to the falls.

There we descended the canyon again and worked our way along the riverbank. Back in the woods, for a time, there was a game path paralleling the water. Spruce brush, boulders and blowdown covered most of the route past the rapids. Walking was difficult enough not to tempt us to try that

Uncle Raymond and cousin Leo on a corduroy bridge near Brantingham.

way with the canoe until someone had been through there with an axe and a crosscut saw, us if necessary.

The river is rough almost all the half-mile from the falls to the site of the Yousey camp. The 1916 New York Oswegatchie Quadrangle shows the camp on the south bank opposite a small brook near which a road, from Star Lake to Aldrich, crosses the Little River. I think we found that brook which, my Uncle Raymond says, was "Sometimes known as Beahan Creek." (Perhaps it was so known by him and his little cousin Bessie.)

Raymond remembered fishing behind a dam and from a corduroy bridge across the river. Jamison describes "a rock reef clear across the stream bed" as "the signal that you have nearly reached the W. edge of the half mile wide private land."

Jamison's rock reef is there. I suspect that it is the remains of the dam and the bridge. But there is little else to suggest that a road once crossed the river there.

We wanted to cross to the camp on the south side of the river but lots of water was pouring through. The river is thirty to forty feet wide there and up to four or five feet deep. It was too chilly for a swim so we left that for next time.

We had a great farewell dinner at the Twin Spruce, which appears to be the first new restaurant in Star Lake in the last fifty years. The french fries and apple pie there are the kind that are worth every bit of their cholesterol, the kind to die for.

As we shook hands to part, Nick said, "It wouldn't take much."

"You want to?"

"With a little help."

"I'll call that guy at the DEC, that Bernie told us about."

"You got to come along, too."

"Let's do it."

This story is a part of our negotiations with the DEC to get rid of those strainers and to cut a portage around the falls of the Little River. If you want to get into the act, speak to Pat Whalen about it. He's the DEC Unit Management Planner for the Little River at 6739 U.S. Highway 11, Potsdam NY 13676. Tell him you would like to make this trip and that you would particularly like to help saw through some of that blowdown.

Appendix A

(Copy of contract between the Beahan Brothers and McDonald Brothers)

Carthage, N.Y.
Sept. 17, 1907

THIS AGREEMENT made today between McDonald Bros. and Beahan Bros. In which Beahan Bros. Agree to cut, skid and deliver to R.R. at Wanakena 1500cds. More or less, spruce and balsam pulpwood.

Said wood to be taken from north side of Cat Mountain or north side of camp built by Wm. Abrams.

Wood to be sound and cut in 4 ft. lengths to be taken larger than 16 inches on a stump.

In consideration McDonald bros. agree to pay Beahan Bros. the sum of $3.62.50 per cord, payments to be made as follows;
$1.75 per cord when wood is piled on roads and balance when wood is delivered at Wanakena.

McDonald Bros. further agree to give Beahan Bros. use of 6pr. Sleighs free of charge. Beahan Bros. are to return goods in as good condition as when received.

McDonald Bros.

Duncan McDonald

Beahan Bros.

Appendix B

The Beahans of Carthage

May 9, 1972

This is a summary of the movements and places lived by Thomas Beahan family of Carthage, N.Y., as well as I remember it—some happenings may be in error or chronologically misplaced, as memory sometimes flutters. Last Sunday Rita Lackey and I were talking of old days and it brought to mind, to me to jot down some of the moves and a few of the happenings. I have left a little space here and there for any notations anyone might want to make.

Raymond Beahan

BIRTHS:—

Thomas xxFrancis Beahan, Antwerp, Feb11, 1865 son of Wm. Henry B. and Rose Anna Pierce B.

((Thomas' family were William, Mary, John Bartholemew (Barty), Margaret (Maggie), and Thomas. Chronog. thus.,as I remember. Dates xxxxxxof birth unknown to me.

xxxxxWillie went away,.perhaps to the west and never heard of again; Mary married Newton Jonas of Great Bend; John married Olivia. asister of Newt's ; Barty never married; Maggie married Gib Wilcox; Tom married, first. Susie Jonas, sister of Newt. she died in a year or two, then he married Minnie Lenore Beahan of Pinckney.

Thomas B. married Minnie L. Beahan on Jan31, 1899, at St. James Catholic Church, Carthage, N.Y.—Rev. Father McCramer.

Minnie was the daughter of Nicholas of Nicholas Gifford and Emma C. Babbit G., lived on a farm in Pinckney, Tug Hill, near Copenhagen—she had one sister, Edith, who married Charley Carpenter.

Children of Thomas & Minnie Beahan:-

Raymond Nicholas— born on Fulton St.,   Carthage April 18, 1900

Genevieve	Carthage Jan. 3, 1902
Lawrence Patrick	Carthage July 21, 1904
Margaret M.	Carthage April 20, 1907
Bernard	Carthage June 26, 1911
Rita	On Maxwell farm near " March 27, 1916

When Thomas and Minnie were first married, I believe that they lived in part of a large brick house, way down, on Alexander St., Carthage; then in a house on Fulton St., near corner of Fulton and N.Washington east side, perhaps the 2nd house from corner. This is where Raymond was born.

In 1901 or 1902 to Aldrich, 36 miles from Carthage, on Carthage & Adirondack R.R. (C. & A.) ——to a log camp in the woods a mile or two east of Aldrich village, Along Little River at point where it is inter-sected by a small trout stream, sometimes known as Beahan's Creek. They (Uncle John, Barty, and Thomas (Beahan Bros.)) had taken a timber cutting and hauling job from Maxwell and Yousey (probably Gus M. father and his son, Fred and Peter Yousey). Uncle John and Aunt Oliva lived in another log camp there and there was a barn and probably a sleeping camp and a root-house. Aunt Oliva's two older children, Leo and Susie, went to Carthage to school, staying with Uncle Newt and Aunt Mary. Bessie (Baba) aunt Oliva's other girl, xxxand I (Raymond) played together. Sometimes, on week-ends and on vacations, Leo/ and Susie and Alton & Rose, (A. & R. were Gib Wilcox's and Maggie B's children; Maggie had died when they were very young and they went to Uncle N's & Aunt M's to live—went by name of Jonas) (the Jonases had had a little boy, Johnny, who had fallen down stairs when a baby and killed) would come up on the train to the camps. We children had good fun wandering the woodlands; Playing around the "bungly tree" a huge, old curly-barked, birch; in the hollow, upper part of a big stump—this was our "balloon——we were up kind of high in it and would look down as we floated away; in summer, the children from Carthage (Leo, S, etc) would have "plays", doing the acting on a "stage" of old boards in the barn—Leo wold sometimes be blackened with burnt cork—some would shoot off a cap pistol. We picked berries; caught trout from the dammed up water of the creek, fishing from the corduroy road or from raft. Some times papa would carry me on his shoulders, hopping from log to log on the water. In the mornings we would often hear the men grinding their axes on the grind-stone or the activity of hitching up the horses.

We had a root house for storing vegetables. One night I went out into it with Uncle John to catch a 'coon which was over the door in root-house. I guess I held the lantern, Uncle John had on leather gloves. In the darkness I could see the 'coon's eyes shining.

Once, I remember, there was a forest fire way back of our camp; the whistle at Aldrich blew (probably the saw-mill whistle) and men came up to fight it. Once, The top of Aunt Oliva camp, at the stove-pipe exit, caught fire. Aunt O. rushed out and called to Uncle John who was working nearby. He stopped his work, looked up reached into his pocket and got his pipe, filled it and lit it, then, went and put out the fire. Uncle John always smoked a clay pipe—he would break it off short when new xxso as to not have it break too short—he smoked Warnick & Brown tobacco. Once, Uncle John wrote a letter to Newt Jonas. Carthage—he addressed the letter, "Nut Jonas".

In the Fall a small party of hunters came to hunt deer, staying at Uncle John's camp—he would guide them; one was a Mr. Parker; one was a Mr. Taft, a preacher, cousin, I believe of Pres. Taft.

On wintry nights I remember being in the camp, mama sewing or doing some work, and I would hear the whistle of the train as it passed thru Aldrich. That was a way- off sound from another world.

We lived in the one camp at Aldrich for 5 years—this woods was virgin timber when we came there. In 1907, the contract being completed we moved to Carthage.

(This is a copy of the first section of a type-written account of the Thomas Beahan family by Raymond Beahan.
The xxxing, spelling and punctuation are his own)

Uncle Raymond Beahan dressed to get married or go to a funeral.

Appendix C

Locke, Cayuga Co. N.Y.

Nov. 13 1905

Dear Friends of "Jolly Camp"

For that is the way I headed my letters when with you. What jolly times we did have indeed. Yes, & how often I have thought of you all these days when I fancy the tracking must have been fine. How is? Was it so? Here it has been ideal deer weather most of the time since I returned. Well my 2 friends & I went to Harrisville & up to Coles but our Fulton and Oswego friends did not come till on Wednesday afternoon & got one fair sized deer. We hunted on A.M. of Thursday then walked to Harrisville & had fine dinner at 12:30 & mash you we were ready for it you bet. M. Cole does not set the table which John Beahan does. Nay, Nay!! Well John, Barty, Tom & the rest there are deer at Coles in there by the river & Fish Creek & Palmer. Last year that same company 12 of them each got a deer. Strange the deer stay there so. Lots of them are taken too.

Mrs. Beahan please say good bye to Mr. and Mrs. Thomas for me. We left so early in the morning that I forgot it. Did not see them. Bart I gave your name to the W.A. Abel Co. in Syracuse & they said they would send you a catalog. Fine men I think.

Well I am right at my work & feel so well thanks in part to the good care I had in the Beahan camp. Now you say what about that horse? Sure Barty well, I am glad to say he is almost well. Thank God! Only think I had written to Mr. Thom to have him skinned. He is more lively than before he was taken sick.

There, it is snowing. It is now 1 P.M. Monday. Remember me to dear little Leona. Have her tell the men they must be sure to call that path by her name. Remember me to all your workmen whom I know. I hope to send you some thing that you may enjoy seeing. Success to you all & thanks again for such a good time. I can't forget that Saturday eve concert Ha! Ha!

Good Bye
Jay Taft

(The Rev. Jay Taft was a cousin to President Taft, according to Beahan family lore. In his letter, he refers to John and Oliva Beahan, Thomas and Minnie Beahan and Bartholomew Beahan. This is copied from Uncle Raymond's hand copy of Rev. Taft's original which the Reverend had typed in blue ink and double-spaced).